AMERICA'S
HOUR OF DECISION

AMERICA'S
HOUR OF DECISION

Crisis Points in National Policy

BY

GLENN FRANK

WHITTLESEY HOUSE
McGRAW-HILL BOOK COMPANY, INC.
NEW YORK AND LONDON
1934

PUBLISHED BY WHITTLESEY HOUSE
A division of the McGraw-Hill Book Company, Inc.

Printed in the United States of America by The Maple Press Co., York, Pa.

TO

GLENN FRANK, Jr.

WHOSE GENERATION WILL BE HEIR
TO
THE WISDOM OR THE FOLLY
OF
OUR CURRENT DECISIONS

CONTENTS

PROLOGUE

THE SACRAMENT OF CHOICE

THE air is everywhere astir with premonitions of profound change in the political, social, and economic life of the United States. A disturbing sense of uncertainty of outcome haunts the national mind. It is impossible confidently to predict the direction this change will finally take.

We may be in for a long retrogression, or we may be on the threshold of renaissance. The blackening of the skies that began in 1929 may have heralded a permanent eclipse of the national genius, or these may be but the gray hours before a social sunrise that will warm and illumine our lives where transient disaster has lately chilled and darkened them.

We are victims of a confused expectancy!

Many Americans, who are sensitively aware that sweeping revisions of policy are imperative if we are to be served instead of starved in this age of plenty, are sincerely fearful that, under the lash of panic fear and the lure of uncritical hope, we may rush into changes that will bring the best in our traditional order of private enterprise and political liberty to a decisive and disastrous end. And they see no matured alternative around which grave doubts do not swarm. These Americans have no personal or political axes to grind by their expres-

[3]

sion of this fear. Their concern is genuine. And they merit more than satire when they voice their doubts.

A few Americans, it may be, with less sincerity of concern, attempt to further personal and partisan interests by branding even the simplest and most obviously sensible suggestion of change as part of some sinister plot to communize the nation. It is pointless to waste words on this Machiavellian minority, for, sooner or later, the bogey-mongers, whether they hail from the ranks of reaction or the ranks of radicalism, are strangled by their own insincerity.

But, whether sobered by calm analysis or swept by faked alarms, the national mind is anxiously speculating on the turn affairs may take in the days ahead. There is everywhere an uneasy sense that the flow of events, both within our own frontiers and throughout the world, is forcing us relentlessly to the sacrament of choice between competing philosophies of the national being.

We are in something of the plight of the priests of Baal when Elijah demanded of them a decision between competing gods.

In one of the most vivid episodes of the Old Testament, the prophet Elijah faced a people divided in loyalty between the worship of Baal, one of the numerous gods of the idolatrous Israelites, and the worship of the Lord who was, to Elijah, the true God. To Elijah, Baal was Illusion, while the Lord was Reality. Impatient at the

indecision of the Israelites, Elijah staged a demon-
stration in which he challenged the followers of
Baal to join him in prayer to their respective gods
to send fire to consume the sacrifices they would
set upon their separate altars. As the record goes,
Baal failed his followers, while the Lord of Elijah
descended in consuming fire. At the outset, Elijah
had said to the wavering Israelites, "How long
halt ye between two opinions? If the Lord be God,
follow him; but if Baal, then follow him." But, as
the record has it, the people answered him not a
word. Later, however, after Baal had ignored the
importunity of his followers, and the flame of
Elijah's Lord had licked up the water-soaked
sacrifice, the halting Israelites cried aloud, "The
Lord, he is the God; the Lord, he is the
God."

As long as the issue was mired in the abstraction
of debate, they wavered. But events finally educated them to a decision.

No other story of ancient scripture or modern
letters quite so accurately describes the dilemma
the time puts to us as this moving recital of how a
prophet faced a people halting between two opinions and insisted that they must make up their
minds about the god to whom they would give
allegiance, that they must really decide what they
believed and act decisively upon their belief. For
we, like the folk around Elijah, are faced with the
necessity of making some major decisions, decisions that will determine the national destiny in

[5]

which the destinies of ourselves and of our enterprises are intimately involved.

Like the followers of Baal, before Elijah forced the issue, we, before the impact of depression sobered us, were content to drift. We were so busy clipping coupons we refused to consider basic issues of national policy. Why bother about the conflicting claims of the Lord and Baal as long as the market was bullish? Maybe a few million Americans were left in the outer darkness that ringed the charmed circle of the prosperous. What of it! The poor we would always have with us! Things, by and large, were going good. Judged by the indices of the economists, we had entered a New Era from which the traditional cyclic ebbs and flows of enterprise had been outlawed. Down with the Cassandras! Up with the Pollyannas! While the joy ride lasted, we tolerated but did not take seriously those Socratic skeptics who all along insisted upon asking where the nation was headed.

It is a different story now. The house of cards collapsed about our ears in 1929. Overnight the enterprise of this age of plenty suffered a stroke of paralysis. And the paralysis stubbornly resists the hundred and one medicines an empirical statesmanship prescribes. A new mood begins to fall over the American mind. The myriad millions begin to lose faith in facile panaceas that put plasters on this and that effect, while basic causes of the disease are left untouched. Here and there leaders who were

[6]

but lately blind begin to realize that decisions more basic than any yet faced must be made. There are, of course, Americans who still see in the situation no more than a chance to rehabilitate outworn economic dogmas and restore to power obsolete political leaderships. But, despite the instances of retarded intelligence still manifest in some political and business circles, events are rapidly educating us to the necessity of a bold clarity of decision on a few basic policies.

The sooner a sense of this necessity sweeps the national mind the better, for there are a few fundamental decisions which, as a people, we must make and make soon if we are to avoid economic chaos, stabilize and make socially viable our industrial system, and through it all preserve a way of life congenial to the American temperament.

If this seems a too excited putting of the case, a cool measurement of the wide chasm that separates the post-war world from the pre-war world will indicate, I think, that it is not.

Before the war, we, along with a growing number of the Western peoples, were committed to a decently definite scheme of values or, at least, to a pattern of foundation principles. There were a few things we believed in profoundly, even if, here and there, we broke with them in practice. There were a few things we felt to be among the fixed foundation stones of our civilization. The superstructure might, in this or that respect, betray disharmony

[7]

with the foundation, but that, we assumed, was a matter to be corrected as we further sharpened our insight and further socialized our outlook.

We believed that democratic self-government, wisely adapted to the diversities of national temperament and tradition and progressively adjusted to the changing circumstances of succeeding generations, was a climactic point in political evolution, that democracy was in the line of historic inevitability, destined to dominate the relations of modern mankind.

We believed that the utmost freedom of life and enterprise consistent with just and reasonable relationships was essential to the safety, the success, and the self-respect of mature peoples.

We believed that the genius we were bringing to bear upon scientific research, technological application, and economic management was leading mankind out of the Death Valley of Scarcity into the Promised Land of Plenty and laying the foundation for an unprecedented enrichment of the lives of the millions.

We believed that individual incentive and individual initiative were fundamental to the continuity of progress, and that, in setting up the necessary safeguards against their prostitution to anti-social ends, the dynamic they give to life and enterprise must not be destroyed.

We believed that science had come that men might have life and that they might have it more abundantly, that science should, therefore, be given

[8]

its head, and the track cleared for its triumphant extension of the productive capacities of our enterprise.

We believed that a stable and significant national life was impossible apart from a soundly conceived and adequately supported system of universal education.

We believed that, however undesirable the sweeping standardizations of a world-state might be, our separate and specialized nationalisms must somehow be orchestrated and brought into a working relationship that would function in terms of the manifest cultural and economic interdependence of the modern world.

These were among the articles of political, social, and economic faith to which, with varying degrees of consecration, we and other peoples of the pre-war West subscribed.

All this is changed now. From one end of the Western world to the other, these articles of faith are philosophically doubted or passionately derided. The slow gains of generations have been set aside in a frantic search for new foundations of national being. Democracy is flouted. Freedom is invaded. Plenty is renounced. Science is betrayed. Education is hamstrung. Religion is tied to the cart tail of the state. Nationalism runs amuck. While politics, as it assumes greater and greater power over our lives, is expressed, not in that sobriety of thought and steadiness of action the time demands, but in distracted agitations which, in Macaulay's

[9]

memorable phrase, resemble "the grinnings and writhings of a galvanised corpse, not the struggles of an athletic man."

This is the backdrop against which the American venture in readjustment must be played out. It is no easy matter to keep the American mind free from the infections that elsewhere run rampant in this feverish interlude while the Western world seeks to experiment its way to a new social equilibrium. The stage-setting of the political and economic play is essentially the same here as it is elsewhere. Change faces tradition and challenges it. Tradition faces change and resists it. It is easy, given the requisite temperament, to follow the lead of the dogmatic reactionary and beat the drums for anything and everything traditional. It is easy, granted the turn of mind, to follow the lead of the dogmatic radical and gamble recklessly with the lives of 125,000,000 Americans as if they were pasteboard pawns in a play at cards. Either path, it seems to me, is likely to land us in the abyss.

The question that emerges from the events of the time is this: Can we ride the storm, and make the revisions of political and economic policy which the effective operation of an age of plenty requires, without subjecting the American order of private enterprise and political liberty to subversive changes that may bring ultimate ruin in the wake of a delusive recovery?

This is the single question into which all other questions of the time lead. The answer that na-

tional action makes to this question will determine
the nature of the national destiny. This is why the
administrative acts of the Roosevelt regime, the
campaign maneuvers of the Republican opposition,
the quality of thought and will that business
leadership brings to the problems of readjustment,
and the corrective impact of an informed public
opinion on all three assume an importance that
has not attached to the management of policy
within the lifetime of any of us now living.

I want, in this brief book, to air this issue with
as much candor and realism as I can muster.
This is in no sense a partisan document. It does not
concern itself with the minutiae of current legislation. And it attempts no judgment on the strategies
of current campaigns. It deals rather with the
broad trends of American life and enterprise as
affected by science, technology, power production,
and the epidemic experimentalism that marks the
politics of the time.

Certain words and phrases run with unavoidable
repetition through all the chapters, words and
phrases that have to do with the contrasted concepts of plenty and scarcity, democracy and
dictatorship, freedom and regimentation, individualism and collectivism, internationalism and
nationalism. Some of these words and phrases have
been worn thin by wide and constant usage since
,1929. I use them because they have become the
coin current of political, social, and economic
discussion. I use some of them, however, in a sense

materially different from the meaning they currently carry. This is particularly true of the sense in which, throughout this study, I speak of our living in an age of plenty and under an economy of plenty. Since this concept is basic to so much of the argument I am concerned to advance, I am taking time here to define what I mean by our economy of plenty.

When I speak of this age of plenty or of our economy of plenty, I do not mean, as some political thinking of the time seems to mean, that we are confronted with a surplus economy, which has brought the possibility of industrial and agricultural expansion virtually to a dead end and made the rationed restriction of production inescapable. The congested surpluses that so gravely concern government are false surpluses. Enough legitimate need exists to absorb every existing surplus and call for a marked expansion of our productive facilities. To feed, clothe, and house the American population adequately would, for instance, seriously overtax our existing productive facilities in these three basic fields. In the sense of latent but clearly feasible capacity, we are in an economy of plenty, but, in no true sense, are we in a surplus economy.

I am aware that, as an immediate problem for the producer, a surplus is a surplus regardless of what caused it. But political or economic statesmanship, concerned with the long-time development of the nation's life and enterprise, must reserve the term surplus production for goods not socially needed instead of using it for goods that are difficult or impossible to sell at the moment.

The inexplicable riddle of contemporary politics is the way in which leadership is formulating policies to fit an assumed surplus economy that does not exist instead of searching for the policies that will release the locked energies of the actual economy of plenty that does exist, in the sense that we have at last learned how adequately to supply human need, even if we have not yet learned how adequately to translate existing human need into effective economic demand.

The implications of this riddle run throughout American life. I have sought, in the chapters to follow, to trace these implications as they affect the principles, motive forces, and instrumentalities of the American tradition of private enterprise and political liberty.

I

THE TEMPER OF THE CROWD

THE temper of the crowd is one of the major
factors with which statesmanship must deal
alike in fair weather and foul. Whether the
historic phase be one of revolution or reaction, the
mass mood is a conditioning force in the formulation of both political and economic policy.

If the phase be one of reaction and the mass mood
a mood of unconcern, statesmanship has a relatively
easy task. Under such circumstances, a do-little-
and-say-nothing leadership may seem the possessor
of a sagacity and strength of which the first breath
of genuine difficulty will show it bereft. We have
seen this happen again and again, alike in political
and in economic fields, during the last ten years,
as we rode the crescendo of a delusive prosperity
and dropped into the diminuendo of depression.
Mushroom monarchs of business, industry, and
finance strutted for a day while the fantastic era of
speculation came to climax, but disaster pricked
the bubble of their supposed astuteness. They were
soon seen to have been men playing in the suburbs
of a situation they did not understand. And, in
politics, presidents and premiers who, with a world-
wide collapse in the immediate offing, refused to

admit its imminence and played cheer-leader to the economic dance of death in which government and business whirled as partners were said to be giving their peoples a stabilizing leadership. They, too, are now seen to have been lacking in that foresight which is one of the fundamentals of great statesmanship.

If the phase be one of revolution and the mass mood a mood of rebellion, statesmanship sails in turbulent seas. If it is to sublimate to productive ends the rebellions of the time instead of surrendering to them, its mind must be free enough to know a valid protest when it hears it, and firm enough to answer it with an action that does not cause more troubles than it cures. It must be supple enough to bend in the wind without breaking, but set deeply enough in reality to stay rooted. It must fashion its policies in conformity with the nature of the age it seeks to rule, and not attempt to impose upon the enterprise of the time arrangements alien to the temper of the people or in conflict with those basic forces which lie beyond politics and give to the thought and work of an epoch their distinctive form.

If the phase be neither reactionary nor revolutionary, but a phase of sudden disarray in the daily enterprise of the people, and the mass mood a mood of bewilderment shot through with an inarticulate resentment that may take an unpredictable turn, the problem of statesmanship becomes extraordinarily difficult. But in such a

[15]

phase, no less than in a phase of reaction or a phase of revolution, statesmanship must keep continuous touch with the temper of the crowd. The great statesman will believe in the crowd without bowing to its idolatries, and serve its needs without catering to its whims, but in any event he must understand its mood if he is not to function in a vacuum and give to policy formulations that strike no response in the hearts of the millions.

What is the current temper of the crowd in the Western world, in general, and in the United States, in particular?

It is important to know this if we are to act effectively in the development of either political or economic policy. And it is quite as important to the business man, industrialist, and financier as to the statesman to know it. For a good stretch of years now there has been going on a steady plebeianization of government throughout the world. The man at the bottom of the pyramid has his finger in the pie as never before. This fact is, in a sense, independent of his formal political status. It is quite as manifest under dictatorship as under democracy. Not even a Mussolini could frown down the masses if he ran Italy solely in the interest of the top 4 per cent of her people. It may be set down as one of the new axioms of the time that the business man who does not devise policies that make for the security of the many as well as the profit of the few will, in the long run, be bankrupt, and the statesman who does not devise policies that make

[16]

for the satisfaction of the masses will, sooner or later, be broken.

It may be said that this means the end of the brilliant performance of the independent genius who, in politics and economics, knows better than the crowd what the long-run interests of mankind require. It may be said that this means a short-sighted autocracy of the average and the slowing to a snail's pace of the enterprise of a nation. I do not think so. But, whether we like it or not, this is the imperative of the age in which we live. The crowd is in control.

Luckily, I think, the peculiar nature of an age of science, technology, and power production is such that it can be kept a going concern only as the human needs of the swarming millions are served adequately. The business of a mass-production age cannot but backfire if a philosophy of the few dominates it. The market of a mass-production age dies if the masses lack ample leisure and adequate income. Only through such mass leisure and mass income is mass consumption possible on anything like the scale our productive capacity indicates. The crowd, if I may say it again, is in control. Science and the machine, not the agitators, have put it in control.

This is why it is important, before we buckle down to more specific considerations, to ask what the current temper of the crowd is. What is it elsewhere in the Western world? What is it in the United States?

The mass mood of the rest of the Western world has relevance to our domestic problem. We are part of Western civilization and, despite the distinctiveness we seek to maintain, are not of necessity immune to the distempers that have raced through the minds of peoples elsewhere in the West. The winds of doctrine that have shaken ancient traditions of government and economic organization in Europe blow across our judgments as well. The waves of popular desire that have been lashed up there beat against our shores also. Apart from the fact that reactions of the mass mind elsewhere may, by contagion, set up like reactions here, the mass mood of the other Western peoples affects the political and economic policies which limit or liberate world trade. And the direction world trade takes for the quarter century ahead is likely to loom larger as a factor affecting our national fortunes than many, in the half-hysterical thinking of the moment, are inclined to admit.

To forget ourselves for the moment, the rest of the Western world is passing through a phase of profound disillusionment. Traditions and folkways that have long served as the stabilizer and scaffolding of men's lives are subjected to a sweeping skepticism that has gone beyond the critical confines of the intellectualists to give direction to the uncritical reactions of the mass mind. Where once men's minds were certain they are now cynical. Where once men were animated by a buoyant confidence that human genius was equal

[18]

to the conquest and control of nature, human nature, and social organization despair now darkens their outlook. Where once great binding beliefs held peoples together in a saving sense of solidarity they now disintegrate into a sordid scramble of individual and class interests. Where once men but criticized the functionings of their major social institutions they now challenge their foundations. Where once men went for guidance to the sober assessments of philosophy they now lend a ready ear to the theatrical screams of passion. In the face of the manifest possibility of plenty in this age of science, technology, and power production, a heightened resentment of wide differentials of wealth arises. We witness a resurgence throughout Europe of the gospel of equality. And hitherto docile masses everywhere seem set to take affairs into their own hands or lodge them in the hands of leaders who speak their language of urgency.

Here and there in Europe we have seen erstwhile stable peoples fall victim to this disillusionment of spirit, dispersion of mind, and determination of will. Determination of will may seem out of place in this trilogy, but, in phases of profound unsettlement, very often the less serene the spirit and the less sure the mind the more savage the will.

We have seen a sober and thoughtful folk like the Germans, with their necks in the noose of an indefensible peace treaty and their backs bent under the weight of post-war obligations they could not carry, make a brave, if futile, attempt to

[19]

build their future upon the foundation of political democracy and a modernized capitalism. But, as post-war months stretched into tragic years, a growing disillusionment with social instrumentalities that were failing to work fell upon the German spirit. The German soul was driven by a deep and honest desire for a political system more effective than the parliamentary democracy of the Weimar constitution was proving, an economic system free at least of the grosser inadequacies of post-war capitalism, and a religious system that would throw the driving power of a spiritual impulse back of the national struggle for recovery and stabilization. The more traditional leaderships seemed powerless to lead the people out of the wilderness of their difficulties. And at length this great people, seduced by madness and mountebankery, followed a Pied Piper of hysteria down the street in seeming disregard of the gamble involved.

Given the mood that has moved so much of Europe in these later years, it has become impossible to predict, on the basis of the historic character of a people, the turn its affairs may take when the normal forms of government and enterprise break down and the traditional leaderships fail to produce popularly satisfactory results. This is an important factor of the world environment in which we must function.

The American situation differs widely from the European situation on many counts, but it has presented stubborn difficulties with which our traditional leaderships have not been accustomed to deal, and it is still crowded with unpredictable possibilities. A swift survey of what has happened to the American temper under the changing fortunes of the last ten years indicates the nature and extent of the difficulties with which American statesmanship must reckon and which American business men, industrialists, and financiers must take into account in their forging of policy for the future.

As I suggested in my *Thunder and Dawn*, which I wrote at the outset of the depression, our national life is now in the fourth phase of a sequence of developments that has before in history brought whole peoples to the social crossroads where decisions affecting their destiny have had to be made. Unless I grossly misread the meaning of the last two decades of American history, four distinct developments have shoved the American social order toward its present critical juncture.

First, old philosophies and old procedures which had long dominated the political, social, and economic life of the United States fell into varying degrees of futility through the failure of American leaderships to keep them progressively adjusted to the new circumstances of this new age of science, technology, and power production.

Second, while these old philosophies and old procedures were falling into futility, new philosophies and new procedures, more alert to the needs and better adapted to the nature of this new age, were being patiently and unobtrusively elaborated by scientists and seers whose historic mission it is to be the unofficial statesmen who, in freedom from the clamor of constituencies and the compulsion to compromise, blaze new trails of thought and action which the official statesmen may later follow if they will.

Third, a long period of manifest maladjustment between the old policies and the new problems of American life ensued, but, despite the heavy hand this maladjustment laid upon the lives of men, the overwhelming majority of Americans clung un-critically to the doctrines of the fathers in matters political and economic.

Fourth, in the wake of the world-wide economic collapse, Americans generally were shaken out of the sterile serenity they had consistently displayed under the pathological prosperity that met so signal an arrest in 1929, with the result that to-day they no longer display reluctance to question even the major assumptions upon which American life and enterprise have long been organized.

It is the mood of this fourth phase, differing so radically from the mood of the three preceding phases, that makes critical the present juncture in American affairs.

In the days of our phantom prosperity, we were sleek and self-satisfied. We were well-fed and wanted nothing so much as to be let alone. We were impatient of those queer persons who were forever raising critical questions about our political, social, and economic policies. As if anything could be wrong with a civilization that was paying such excellent dividends!

The result of all this was that we turned deaf ears to the advocates of political, social, and economic readjustments that might well have moderated, if not averted, the ruinous retardation that has held so much of our enterprise in virtual suspense since 1929. The American mind seemed stubbornly resistant to new ideas. The boat was sailing in calm seas. Why rock it with reconsiderations of policy!

Almost the sole exception to this reluctance to reconsider the orthodoxies of our traditional habits was the lush growth of bootleg religions and the rise of an apostolate of fakirs who led thousands of otherwise intelligent Americans to believe that, in their wistful quest for the deeper meanings of existence, they could suck the juices of a living gospel from the dead rinds of ancient superstitions or the green stalks of bogus psychologies. It may be that mankind will always rebel in this irrational manner against an era that becomes so exclusively absorbed in the goods and chattels of a crass prosperity. At any rate, aside from this gullible embracement of improvised religions, and its perfect willingness to scrap machines and methods of production in even early stages of obsolescence, the American mind betrayed a baffling immunity to new ideas as long as the economic skies were bright. And even the new religionists, with fat pay

[23]

checks in hand and seated at the wheels of fast cars, closed their minds to political and economic reconsiderations.

This nation-wide mood of reluctance to reconsider was not confined to the big speculators or restricted to men with the highest stakes in the easy profits of the time. Even the little man was drunk with dreams of the poker profits he hoped to reap from speculation. It was a temper of the crowd, not the trickery of the few, that gave to this phase its peculiar character. It would be difficult, I think, to name even one socially productive new idea respecting political or economic policy that can be said to have swept the mass mind during the prosperity cycle.

An old Scotchman, seeking to account for this seeming inability of a new idea then to fire the mass mind, said, "The heather was wet." When the heather is wet, fires do not, of course, sweep easily across the fields. But to-day the situation is the exact reverse. The heather is not wet. The heather is dry. Disillusionment has done its perfect work. The man in the street, along with the man in the furrow, is straining at the leash of old dogmas of politics and economics that have failed to keep hunger from his stomach, cold from his body, and fear from his heart. The tethers of a thousand traditional loyalties have slipped during the last five years as men have watched the very ground-stakes of their social order loosen. And from one end of the United States to the other men are to-day fumbling blindly for some lead out of the blind alleys into which blind leaderships led them.

Such a mood is at once a grave danger and a great opportunity. A grave danger if irresponsible demagogy dominates it! A great opportunity if responsible statesmanship directs it! In its present mood the mass mind is willing to follow responsible statesmanship. It would prefer to follow responsible statesmanship. It *may* follow irresponsible demagogy. The turn that mass judgment may take will depend upon the nature of the results statesmanship is able to achieve without undue delay.

The mass mind was willing to take counsel of its patience while a Roosevelt gathered power unprecedented into his hands and cut the red tape that normally binds government to the hitching post of inaction. But, unless I fail utterly to sense its present mood, it will not unduly prolong its patience. There is a latent impatience moving restlessly close under the surface of the liberal patience Americans generally have displayed during the difficult days of the last five years. The mass mind expects permanently productive results to follow the freedom to act which its mood made Congress make possible as the Roosevelt regime swung into action in the early months of 1933. And, let us speak plainly, the mass mind expects something more than a Red Cross statesmanship that momentarily salves the economic wounds of the time and subsidizes into transient silence a vast army of Americans for whom no secure place is open in the normal enterprise of the economic order. It expects careful but courageous readjustments of our political, social, and economic policies that will enable us to take full human advantage of the fruits of this new age of science, technology, and power production.

It was for this, and this alone, that we adjourned so much that is traditional in our democracy. It was for this, and this alone, that we set up a crisis government under which a Roosevelt is given in peace time powers far beyond the powers given a Wilson in war time. And this mass mind will hold this crisis government to strict accountability. If the fruits of this freedom to act, which the mass mood made possible, should fail visibly to ripen or, when ripened, should prove unpalatable to Americans generally, the mass mind will turn inevitably to an alternative leadership. And the danger is that it might be none too discriminating in its selection of the alternative.

This mass mind might go dangerously far to the right. Strained by an excess of novelty in Rooseveltian policy, it might turn in blind reaction against everything experimental, and gamble a living future on dead doctrines. It might lodge the leadership of the nation in the hands of men who would stubbornly refuse to see that when a people emerges, as we have emerged, from an economy of scarcity into an economy of plenty, its political, social, and economic arrangements must be made to fit the scale and tempo of the new order of production. A national leadership of this sort would, in the end, mean national suicide. It could not but mean the reenactment a few years hence, on a doubled or trebled scale, of the disastrous depression that has so nearly rocked our social order to its foundation.

We must accustom ourselves to the fact that there is danger on the right as well as danger on the left. A blindly reactionary leadership assuming control of the United States at this juncture would, if it wanted to retain power for long, find itself strongly tempted, if not actually compelled, to suspend the traditional processes of democratic self-government, although the suspension might, with us, be ingeniously camouflaged. Reaction and representative government, as we have known it, will not be able to coexist in the United States in the years ahead. The danger to constitutional self-government is quite as great from the reactionary right as from the radical left. The reasons for this are, I think, quite clear.

In the first place, the crowd, let me repeat, is in control. The plebeianization of government, to which I have already referred, has put power in the hands of the millions. And no class has ever in history conquered political power without seeking to use this power to better its lot. It may, therefore, be set down as inevitable that the American millions will increasingly seek to better their economic lot through the use of their political power. This means that, in the future, the only leadership that can count upon sustained popular support will be a leadership that makes economic satisfaction and economic security for the masses available to the maximum point of possibility.

In the second place, alongside this plebeianization of government, power production has marched across industry with seven-league boots. The triple ministry of science, technology, and power has, for the first time in history, made this mass satisfaction and mass security quantitatively possible. But this mass prosperity, which is at last possible, will not become a socially established fact until leadership substitutes an economics of plenty for the economics of scarcity that still colors and controls the major part of the governmental, industrial, and financial thinking of the United States.

In the third place, a blindly reactionary leadership, with its congenital reluctance to break with anything traditional, will never blaze the trail to a new economics of plenty. But it is only through a responsibly elaborated economics of plenty that the modern economy of science, technology, and power production can be kept a going concern, and it is an economics of plenty that the American millions, with their resistless political power, will increasingly insist upon.

In summary, then, any leadership that cannot and does not deliver a workable economics of plenty will be unable to retain power if the millions are left with their political leverage. This cannot but mean that a blindly reactionary leadership, failing to readjust the old economic policies to the new economic processes, will be driven to suspend the normal procedures of democratic self-government as far as possible, for it simply cannot count on continued support from the masses in a social order that harbors both democracy and mass production. It will seal the hatches on freedom of speech, press, and assembly. It will seek to make the school system its press agent. It will try to annex the pulpit as an ally. It will more and more resort to naked force. It will become a dictatorship in fact even if it does not dictate the color and cut of the shirts of its followers. It will lift its will to the level of law and remake the state into the instrument of its desire.

If mass judgment should, in rebound from what seems to it to have been an excess of experimentation, turn too far to the right, the alternative leadership it selects may well prove but the advance agent of revolution. It has been so throughout history. It will be so again.

The mass mind might, on the other hand, turn dangerously far to the left. In a time of incredible difficulty, mass judgment is at the mercy of short-range interests. Even under normal conditions, the crowd is more likely to think in split seconds than in centuries. Millions have lately learned to nurse at the breasts of government. They will not lightly submit to being torn from this source of sustenance unless a productive leadership invests the normal enterprise of the nation with a new assurance. It is not that the average American prefers relief to reemployment. He does not. And he has an uneasy sense that there is something abnormal and impermanent about this Niagara-like flow of federal funds into direct subsidy and the masqueraded relief of made-work. He would feel easier about the future if he and his fellows were happily at work in a normalized industry and agriculture. But the disaster of the last five years has left him reluctantly skeptical of private leadership. And there is living in his memory the fear that froze his heart before this unprecedented prodigality of public leadership came into the picture. This is anything but a revolutionary mood, but, under certain circumstances, it might lead this average American very far to the left.

If the mass mind of the United States should ever go revolutionary, it will be on the basis of an excessively simplified reaction. If the Roosevelt regime should fail to lead the nation to a restored and rectified economic life in which the rank and file of Americans might feel reasonable security, if the very prodigality and nature of its expenditures should, in the end, freeze instead of prime the pump of enterprise, bringing the economic drive of the nation virtually to a dead stop, with the national credit for these expenditures drying at its source, the mass mind might, without thinking its action through, turn to a more political rather than a less political path out of its difficulties. A stagnant

[30]

economic life would not tend to turn the masses to private economic leadership for salvation. Their short-range interests would tend to obscure long-range considerations. How could they be sure of breakfast tomorrow morning? To men with this sort of question on their lips, constitutionality becomes a cold issue. They might assume that, if government could not tax and borrow its way to protection of mass interests, they would as well take over the economic machine and try their hand at running it on the basis of the really new deal of a profitless economy that produces for use rather than for sale.

I do not say that this shift to the revolutionary left is probable. I do not think it is. But it is wilful self-delusion to assume that it is impossible. I do not say that the facile experimentalism of the Roosevelt regime will be followed by a blindly reactionary leadership. I do not think it will. But, again, it is wilful self-delusion to assume that it is impossible. And it is self-delusion of this sort that has, again and again in phases of unsettlement, landed nations either in the blind reaction that precedes revolution or in the bold revolution that follows unsuccessful reform.

The one thing I feel confident in predicting about the turn American mass judgment will take in the next five to ten years is that it cannot be predicted. We, along with the peoples of Europe, have moved into the zone of unpredictability.

[31]

We do not want either a reactionary leadership that but postpones revolution or a radical leadership that precipitates revolution. We want a statesmanship of intelligent readjustment that provides a permanent alternative to revolution. It is with the animating principles of this sort of leadership, as it wrestles with the problems of democracy, freedom, the economic supply, the social implications of science and education, the function of politics in the affairs of the people, the role of religion in the national life, and the relation of American enterprise to the rest of the modern economic world, that the chapters to follow deal.

II

DEMOCRACY FLOUTED

A DELIBERATE and dramatic secession from democracy has everywhere marked the post-war politics of the Western world. Even those democracies that have not gone openly bankrupt and made formal assignment of their political liberties to some *de jure* or *de facto* dictator have seen the democratic dogma corroded by cynical doubt of its fitness to direct an age at once so intricate and so insecure.

It is a mistake to assume that this epidemic resort to dictatorship has been but a by-product of the chaos into which affairs fell while the nations stupidly engaged in the cooperative suicide of war. Even before war had bled the race white of its old self-reliance, and quite aside from the impetus post-war chaos gave to the seizure and centralization of power the world around, there was a growing conviction in the minds of many that democracy was not up to the job of administering an age of science, technology, and power production. Democracy may have been admirably adapted to the administration of an age in which the scale of enterprise was small, the relationships of life simple, and the tempo of development slow, but, in the modern industrialized world, the scale of enterprise is vast, the relationships of life complex, and the tempo of development swift. Such a world, so the contention ran, demands a stronger leadership than the elections of democracy will commonly call to power or the legislatures of democracy normally tolerate.

The alarming instabilities of the post-war period brought this anti-democratic conviction out of the library of the political philosopher into the arena of political action. Here, there, and yonder it has found varied expression. Here it expresses itself in a proletarian dictatorship that is frankly a class government. There it expresses itself in a more personal dictatorship that disputes the necessity of any class struggle for power, asserts as indefensible any class monopoly of privilege, and purports to merge the separate interests of all classes in the single interest of the state. Yonder it grows, subtly but lushly, under the cover of emergency leaderships that may themselves still adhere in theory to the democratic dogma.

The destiny of democracy in the United States will, in my judgment, depend entirely upon our success or failure in solving the economic problem. If we can now move with reasonable rapidity toward a soundly based and widely distributed economic well-being, essential democracy is not likely to be seriously challenged or successfully supplanted in this generation. But whether we are to succeed or fail in solving the economic problem is still on the lap of the gods as I write this in the middle months of 1934. For all our brave whistling in the dark, we are still far from out of the woods.

Anything less than a complete thawing out of the fountains of enterprise, more or less frozen for the last five years, will put the American tradition of democratic self-government in definite jeopardy. If, when the roaring mountain stream of federal spending and federal subsidy begins to dry up at its source, the private enterprise of the nation remains sluggish or stalled, the American millions will lend a ready ear to drastic alternatives. If recovery comes too slowly, a growing impatience with the traditional forms and functions of government will manifest itself. If we achieve a fair measure of recovery, but, in the achieving, perpetuate the old inequities and inefficiencies of the pre-depression order, recovery will be transient and insecure, popular satisfaction will be short-lived, and democracy's judgment day will be but postponed. Democracy is not invested with any inevitable immortality. Toward the end of his life, the late Lord Bryce ventured the judgment that there were few countries in which the freedom we associate with democracy seemed safe for the century ahead. "When the spiritual oxygen which has kept alive the attachment to liberty and self-government in the minds of the people becomes exhausted, will not the flame burn low and flicker out?" he asked. This is a question we may well ask ourselves as we attempt to assess the American outlook.

The disruptive aftermath of the war and the muddling mismanagement of so much of our economic enterprise, which ended in the disaster of 1929, seriously depleted the spiritual oxygen which, for a century and a half, had kept alive in the minds of the American masses an attachment to liberty and self-government. If now we fail effectively to liquidate the economic hangover from the war and to deal decisively and dependably with the problem of a soundly based and widely distributed economic well-being, this already depleted supply of spiritual oxygen will be utterly exhausted, and democratic self-government may well disappear from the face of this continent as the masses, in despair and under demagogic leaderships arising to batten on their despair, surrender to the delusion of dictatorship.

Democracy has died before in history. And peoples that had known it and prized it seemed not sorry to see it go. When popular government flickered out in ancient Greece and Rome, nobody thought of reviving it. All this may happen again on this continent in this generation. I am convinced that no price we may have to pay to prevent this will be too high, for, despite its manifest weaknesses, democracy is, in the long run, both safer than and superior to dictatorship, despite the swift efficiencies some dictators may seem to bring to phases of emergency.

For a decade or more, we have thoughtlessly assumed that, for any but fair weather, dictatorship, as a working procedure, has the edge on democracy. And, in the midst of what seemed our fumblings, we have looked enviously at the cinema Napoleons who have cracked the whip of a totalitarian leadership over their peoples. What we need is a dictator! This ran, for a time, with the recurrence of a refrain through the talk at our dinner tables and consistently climaxed the debates of relaxed business men in the club cars of crack trains heading into Washington. We are beginning to repent this mood.

The cycle of dictatorship has run long enough in Europe to prove that there is no magic in it, save as some dictator happens to be an intrinsically great leader for some critical hour of transition. And its long-run liabilities begin to emerge. I venture the prediction that the historian will look back upon the decade and a half from the end of the war, which has been considered a kind of twilight hour for democracy, as a period in which, after much confusion of judgment, dictatorship revealed its inevitable weakness and democracy proved its inherent strength.

On things that matter most, the human race seems stubbornly determined not to learn from ancestral experience. To whatever Intelligence may observe us from the cosmic side-lines, it must seem incredible that the long record of historic experience has not, by now, convinced mankind of the futility of force as a solvent of social difficulties. The slump of so many civilized moderns into

[37]

a philosophy of dictatorship shows that it has not.

I approach with profound sympathy the instances in which, since the war, harassed peoples have chosen transient dictatorship in preference to the tragic anarchy of governments which, in the midst of panic disintegration and lacking the capacity to govern, let run unharnessed the wild horses of conflicting interests. The intricate and interdependent life of a modern nation cannot tolerate non-government by stampede. But this is something quite apart from the fashionable turning of tired radicals and impatient liberals to the alluring possibility of taking a short-cut to the triumph of their desires. It is this latter that presents a problem with definite and, in my judgment, dangerous implications for the American future. The lure of dictatorship in a phase of unsettlement makes strange bedfellows. Since 1929, we have seen the most conservative business men and the most radical theorists alike flirt with the notion of dictatorial direction as a way out of our difficulties. That they have differed about the nature of dictatorship that would be most desirable does not change the similarity of impulse that has moved their minds.

When the fever of these days has subsided, we shall see that this wistful admiration of the flourish of dictators was a delusion, and that this insistent cry for action without the seemingly endless discussion of democratic procedure was the cry, not of strong men, but of weaklings. It is the business men who were blind when the economic tides were running high and the liberals who did not know what to do when they had a chance to govern who have most easily surrendered to the lure of dictatorship. Both, a bit ashamed of their record for leadership, are looking for a short-cut to action that will relieve them of the exacting demands that leaders who truly lead must meet.

The liberalism of flexible intelligence was never lower in favor than it has been since 1929. The god of force finds his altars crowded with communicants newly converted to his gospel, but the men of stablest intelligence and strongest will are not kneeling with them. To them, it is incredible that, in the face of historic experience, modern men should still believe that force, unchecked by wide counsel, can govern wisely and well. And yet even the cult of violence has a crowded and growing membership recruited from all kinds and conditions of men from the reactionary right to the radical left. The men who believe that good is gained by war. The men who dream of social salvation by revolt. The men who make and break strikes by force. The men who guard righteousness with tar and feathers. The men who play nurse maid to their neighbor's mind with censorships. The men who become both judge and executioner by self-appointment and travesty justice in lynching bees. These and a host of like adherents to the cult of violence combine to create the soil out of which dictatorships spring.

Despite this madness of the moment, which has contrived to convince multitudes of men that it is the triumph of sanity and strength, it seems to me that four propositions lie so plainly on the surface of the social record of mankind that he who runs may read.

First, force is no final protection to institutions. The force of inquisitors has never saved the church from heresy. The violence of czars has never saved empires from revolution. The censorship of statesmen has never saved nations from radicalism.

Second, force cannot stop the march of ideas. An idea let loose in the world cannot be recalled. It has an immortality all its own. The man who has thought an idea can be imprisoned, but the idea he has thought will slip through the bars and fly on unseen wings through closed doors. Hemlock could kill Socrates, but it left his idea alive. The cross killed Jesus, but his idea went winging round the world.

Third, force cannot compel the agreement of the unconvinced. It is possible through terrorism to compel men to seem to respect ideas they do not believe, but not even terrorism can compel them to believe that the ideas are respectable. The call of comfort is loud, and men tend to grow soft under the seductions of civilization, but the seeds of martyrdom are still hidden in the hearts of men.

And, as the cycle of dictatorship runs on in Europe, we shall see a growing army of unconvinced men face imprisonment and death for their ideas.

Fourth, force does not, in the long run, destroy the morale of the opposition. Force from the outside tends rather to drive men in to a common center of devotion. It is not the disruptive factor it is assumed to be. It makes for cohesion in the camp of the enemy.

The social record of mankind supports neither the reactionary in his belief that the violence of repression insures peace nor the radical in his belief that the violence of revolt insures progress. Unless the historians have played us false by keeping the facts from us, force is a last-resort weapon with limited function. It is too much trusted alike by red radicals and red reactionaries.

Before the current vogue of strong governments set in, we in the United States were asking ourselves certain questions as the news of successive days brought us stories of lynchings, of the iron-handed action of industrial police, of black-lists of supposed reds compiled by daughters of a revolution, of strikes and lockouts, of legislative directions to teachers of science, and the like.

Can the difficult dilemma of racial relations be met with fagot and rope?

In the vexed field of industrial relations, can the militia be made a substitute for management or the swashbuckling of private police take the place of statesmanlike industrial leadership?

Is it worthy of a mature people to leave the determination of industrial policy to an ordeal of battle between competing armies of employers and employees?

Is the effort of black-list compilers to standardize opinion a brave protection of permanent values or the blind unwillingness of the thoughtless to consider the readjustment of old policies to new circumstances?

Can a people save its culture from becoming but the rotting corpse of dead outlooks if it makes the voice of science echo the vote of the majority?

How long may a social order expect to retain its veracity if its laboratories must take orders from its legislatures?

The initiating source of all these questions was a growing skepticism in the minds of intelligent Americans of force as an instrument of social control. We were apparently making some headway against the cult of compulsion. After a sordid flurry, we had turned thumbs down on Ku-Kluxism. The passion to hunt heretics, which in the early twenties expressed itself in a theological vendetta that distracted men's minds from honest worship, had died down. Black-list compilers, save for the professional patriots who lived by the craft, became a bit self-conscious and apologetic. Both union leaders and industrialists thought twice before calling a strike or ordering a lockout, knowing that, with each successive year, such action won less and less popular favor if taken under any save the gravest provocation. Honest opposition to tendencies that smacked of militarism had become more nearly possible without provoking the suspicion of disloyalty or the sneer of impracticality. These were among the signs, meager though they were, of a return to reliance on reason as a guiding principle of social management.

Among Western peoples who had so largely lost confidence in their own capacity to manage their own affairs, we seemed set to retain and renew the essentially pacific philosophy of science and self-government to which America in her saner moments has always adhered. But, as the depression deepened our difficulties, signs cropped out in the temper and talk of the people to indicate a possible backsliding from this philosophy. Could we not find ways to short-circuit the lumbering processes of our democracy and get in the United States some of the decisiveness and drive that dictators seem to possess and to generate? This was obviously a question born of stress and strain. It was, in many instances, never put into words, but merely hovered over and haunted the quiet wondering of troubled Americans. It was not that anybody wanted a dictator, but that everybody wanted relief from the increasingly difficult social and economic situation.

It was this mood that made so easy the lodging of extensive and extraordinary powers in the hands of the President at the outset of the Roosevelt regime. The centralization of extraordinary powers in the executive during an emergency is a special problem calling for a special judgment apart from the broad judgment I am seeking to express on dictatorship and democracy as permanent procedures. But, even to the minds of men who concur in the necessity of emergency grants of extraordinary powers, the exercise of these emergency powers raises fundamental questions that involve long-range values. It is not a simple matter to confine the effect of emergency programs to emergency periods. In utter absence of any deliberate intent, emergency programs may, in a few swift months, remake for a generation to come the attitude of a people toward government.

The after-effect of emergency programs may not be so sweeping and subversive as the ancient historian Polybius traced in the life of ancient Rome. "And hence," he wrote, "when by their foolish thirst for reputation they [the political leaders] have created among the masses an appetite for gifts and the habit of receiving them, democracy, in its turn, is abolished and changes into a rule of force and violence. For the people, having grown accustomed to feed at the expense of others and to depend for their livelihood on the property of others, as soon as they find a leader who is enterprising, but is excluded from the honors of office by his penury, institute the rule of violence." The after-effect of emergency programs may not, as I say, be so sweeping, but a people can easily come out of an emergency, in which government

[44]

has acted bravely and generously, with a frankly
unhealthy reliance on government. Unhealthy, that
is, unless the whole philosophy of private enterprise and political liberty is obsolete. I do not
think it is. On the contrary, its validity grows, I
think, with the growing complexity of the modern
world.

The greater the complexities of an age, the
broader should be the base of judgment upon
which its policies are built. The complexities of our
age are limitless. The capacities of its leaders are
limited. Less than at any time in human history,
therefore, can we afford to put all our eggs in one
basket. Less than at any time in human history can
we afford to bully into silence the voice of corrective
criticism, intimidate minority opinion, and give
unquestioned right-of-way to the green dogmatisms
of politics and economics that sprout so lavishly
from the improvisings of crisis-driven statesmen.
And yet this is to-day happening the world around
wherever the minds of men have been hypnotized
by the glamorous promise and grim discipline of
dictatorship. The very intricacy of modern problems, which has been made one of the major
arguments against democracy, is, in the deepest
sense, the supreme argument for democracy.

The cardinal strength of democracy is that it
broadens the base of judgment upon which policy
is built. All of us, with varying degrees of effect,
can chip in on the discussion that determines
policy. The cardinal weakness of dictatorship is

that it narrows the base of judgment upon which policy is built. Policy is determined solely by the dictator and his particular brand of expert adviser.

The greatness of a civilization is measurable by the capacity of its people and of its government to tolerate and turn to productive use an utterly free enterprise of criticism. We may reread with profit the speech Socrates made at the trial that resulted in his execution, for this classic trial vividly dramatized the issue of the broadening versus the narrowing of the base of judgment upon which the policies of a people are to be built. For a while the ancient Greek civilization was a great and glowing civilization, but one day it suddenly shriveled into littleness and killed its major critic, the skeptical Socrates. By that blunder ancient Greece proved that a people cannot have a thin skin and a great soul, and demonstrated for all time that a government cannot hope to endure unless it knows how to build its policies upon the double foundation of the cooperation and competition of the widest possible variety of judgments.

"If you put me to death," said Socrates to the Athenians who were clamoring for his execution, "you will not easily find another man to fill my place. God has sent me to attack the city, as if it were a great and noble horse which was rather sluggish from its size, and which needed to be aroused by a gadfly. And I think that I am the gadfly that God has sent to the city to attack it,

[46]

for I never cease from settling upon you, and rousing, and exhorting, and reproaching each man of you all day long. You are vexed, as drowsy persons are, when they are awakened, and of course you could easily kill me with a single blow, and then sleep on undisturbed for the rest of your lives, unless God were to care for you enough to send another man to arouse you."

The Athenians did not take his advice. Socrates was sentenced to die by drinking a cup of hemlock. Would it not be easier to build Athenian policy if fewer such dissenters were forever stirring the waters of discussion? The Athenians thought they were merely getting rid of a disturber of their peace. What they were really doing was drowning a whole civilization in one small cup of hemlock. And, through all the centuries since, in times of stress, peoples have been tempted to repeat this Athenian act of social suicide either through the execution of critics or through the excessive centralization of policy-making. It is a gesture that seems to suggest strength at a time when government is secretly fearful that the difficulties of the time may prove too much for it.

It is one of the major delusions of this disintegrate time that the need of the hour is strong government. It is not strong government that we need so much as wise government, government invested with the virtues of insight, dignity, justice, moderation, tolerance, knowledge, and an acute sense of social values.

[47]

Wise governments draw men into authentic loyalty to their purposes. Strong governments drive men into an artificial lip-service to their slogans. Wise government must have wide soils in which to sink its roots. Strong government can build a brief interlude of power on the clever strategies of a clique. Dictatorship offers us the quickest path to strong government. Democracy offers us the surest path to wise government. Dictatorship is founded on fear and faith. Democracy rests upon leadership and popular understanding. Democracy is admittedly impotent in an hour of crisis if leadership is derelict and popular understanding darkened, but its basic concept is sounder than the concept of dictatorship.

If this is true, as I think it is, the problem confronting us is not the renunciation of democracy but its revision in order that it may function more effectively in these disheveled hours of transition from old to new circumstances of life and enterprise. I content myself with four suggestions respecting this necessary revision of democratic procedure to the end that popular government in the United States may match the immediate efficiencies of dictatorship without surrendering the intrinsic superiorities of democracy.

First, we should recognize the necessity and establish a fixed procedure for crisis government for phases of emergency.

Second, we should redefine the respective roles of the legislature and the executive.

[48]

Third, we should fix for all time the function of the expert in a self-governing democracy.

Fourth, we should make specific provision for the adequate training of able public servants.

A vast mass of critical judgment to the contrary notwithstanding, I do not believe that the current situation has invalidated the democratic philosophy of government. I do not believe that events make necessary any revolutionary reconsideration of the foundations of our national being. I think, however, that events have made necessary certain major revisions of democratic procedure. I have suggested four such revisions which I want now to consider in turn.

In the first place, we should, I think, establish a fixed procedure for what Lindsay Rogers terms crisis government for periods of emergency. To anticipate and to discount crises is a mark of maturity in a person or in a people. We cannot always anticipate the policy a crisis may make imperative. We can anticipate the sort of procedure that will make possible the promptitude of action necessary in a crisis and, at the same time, provide against the unnecessarily extensive dismantling of democracy that often accompanies hastily improvised emergency legislation. It is possible also, by forethought, to throw sounder safeguards around the return to normal procedure, when the crisis passes, than are included in the average emergency arrangements formulated in the haste and hysteria of a critical situation.

[49]

When this sweeping collapse came to the enterprise of the world, weak governments saw in the situation a choice between disintegration and dictatorship. Nation after nation chose dictatorship. Disintegration faced us as it faced lesser nations elsewhere in the world. Our government was not weak, but its ways were ill-adapted to the task of dealing with a crisis so grave. And it is not, I should like to insist in passing, any indictment of democracy to admit that its normal procedures are not designed to deal with crises of the magnitude this world-wide depression assumed. A less stable people might have gone the way of dictatorship. We made no revolutionary change in the basic structure of our government. We chose instead temporarily to adjourn some of the more deliberate procedures of legislation and to lodge extraordinary powers in the national leadership for the period of the emergency.

Since then varied forces of opposition have discreetly but determinedly criticized this move as a subtle assault upon democratic self-government. I find myself at variance with much that the national leadership has done with its emergency powers, but the wisdom and necessity of granting to the national leadership extraordinary powers in the midst of emergency cannot, in my judgment, be justly disputed. In no other way can democracy deal effectively with crises of major magnitude. And, if democracy can know when to adjourn and when to reassemble its normal procedures, it thereby proves its superiority to dictatorship, for, in so doing, democracy secures all the short-time advantages of dictatorship without incurring its long-time liabilities.

This technique of crisis government should not, however, be left to the improvisings and intrigues of an hour of incredible worry when the national mind is at wit's end. It should be a matured technique held ready for the moment of emergency.

We know that we cannot take the phenomena of ebb and flow out of the economic life of the modern world. Not even the most tightly planned economy, from which the unpredictable factor of democratic politics had been eliminated, could command brains enough and control enough factors to rid enterprise of ups and downs. Crises will continue their intermittent visitations. This will prove inevitable in any but a static society whose energies may be wholly controllable because they are so severely constricted. A dynamic society cannot escape the fact of surge and setback that seems inseparable from the living disorder of growth which, for all its casualties, invests life and enterprise with a stimulant challenge that utter certainty could never provide.

Life and enterprise in the United States are more complex and less tractable than the ambitious apostles of planning seem to realize. But crisis always tempts men, whose hands are for the moment on the levers of power, to oversimplify their problem and attempt a regularization of the future

[51]

by extending into normal times many of the methods and mechanisms called into being by the abnormal conditions of crisis. At the end of every war, political leadership flirts with the idea of adapting to the administration of peace time the formulas that gave to government the sense of precision and power in war time. At the end of every depression, pressure comes to project into the era of restoration the control devices that crisis made necessary. But plans made in the midst of panic are not likely to fit the radically different requirements of a phase of calm. The problem is different. It is elementary that policy must be different.

As a crisis draws to its close, however, if the crisis leadership has been successful, the situation is weighted in favor of its proposals. The masses will always listen uncritically to the man who has pulled them out of a hole. Even if he has not really pulled them out of a hole, but has made them more comfortable in the hole some preceding leadership dug for them, they will listen uncritically to his plans for the future.

This is why it is important that the technique for the mobilization and demobilization of crisis government be a fixed procedure formulated well in advance of the coming of crisis and without the distortion crisis effects in the thinking of even the ablest leaders. Unless we are ready to risk the junking of the whole concept of private enterprise and political liberty in the enthusiasm of the ending of some war or depression, we should bring to the elaboration of a procedure for the entrance and exit of crisis government quite as much care as the framers of the Constitution brought to the invention of those deliberate limitations on official power which, although they have at times slowed down the adaptation of American government to manifest social change and thrown unmerited protection around anti-social interests, have nevertheless safeguarded the root principle of democratic self-government and saved us from a thousand ventures in hastily conceived change.

In the second place, we should, I think reconsider the respective roles of the legislature and the executive in American government and effect a reallocation of functions between the two. In the United States, as in Europe, some of the basic procedures of parliamentary democracy are not adapted to the administration of a vast, complex, and swiftly moving national life. And, if we want to lay the ghost of dictatorship, we must revamp the techniques of democracy in terms of the scale, complexity, and tempo of the affairs it must to-day administer. This revamping need not, in my judgment, be revolutionary in its nature or involve the surrender of that popular control which is the essence of democratic self-government. An important part of this imperative revamping is, I think, an intelligent readjustment of the roles of legislature and executive.

We must stop the inexpert intrusion of legislators into the detailed aspects of legislation and the intricate processes of administration. We must restrict legislative bodies to the charting of broad paths of policy, to the setting up of the goals that the needs of the inarticulate millions require that we reach, and to a critical checking up on the results of administration.

We must lodge greater detailed power and wider discretion in the executive. In so doing we shall not be creating a dictator. The right of review and the power of recall will still rest with us and with our representatives. The executive power is uniquely in the spotlight. When it runs amuck, we can get at it, as we cannot get at the hydra-headed power of the legislature when it falls victim to caprice or corruption.

The traditional relation of Congress to the President and his administrative colleagues, of state legislatures to governors and officers of state, was wise and workable in the early phase of the national development. The problems of government were then few and negative. The problems of government are now multitudinous and positive. We have passed the point at which the unspecialized good judgment of the mine run of even able representatives can effectively dictate, through the give-and-take of legislative debate, the intimate details of legislation for the management of the vast, complex, and swiftly moving life of the United States. We can strengthen the executive direction of government and throw greater responsibility for the initiation of legislation on the executive without scuttling the principle of popular rule. As long as

[54]

the legislature retains the ultimate power to say in which direction policy shall go, ably maintains a critical audit of the acts of the executive, and serves as a forum for the airing of grievances and the informed discussion of basic principles, it is doing the utmost that a miscellaneous body of elected representatives can safely be trusted to do in an age in which the problems of society are complex and the functions of government positive.

In the third place, we should, I think, fix the function of the expert in American government and make permanent provision for his proper correlation with legislative and executive leadership. Aside from the use of expert personnel in the strictly scientific services of government, we cannot be said to have a national policy respecting the role of the expert in government. Expertness in relation to the formulation of policy has been, from time to time, bootlegged into government as brain trusts and back-door advisers without portfolio. This is not enough. Effective government in the midst of modern complexity is impossible apart from the service of the expert, but his employment must not depend upon the whims of successive administrations, and he must not be set at tasks for which both his temper and his training unfit him.

There can, I take it, be no effective dispute of the necessity of a fact-basis for politics. Unless statesmanship rests upon a scientific study of the causes of social problems and a statistical study of the results of social policies, government must inevitably become the plaything of the demagogue, particularly in a civilization as complex and technical as ours. The statesman must maintain a working alliance with the expert. And he must leave the expert free to follow the facts, for, when the expert is converted into a retained attorney for the dogmas of a party, he stultifies himself and becomes a liability instead of an asset to government.

To confront a nation with a tax bill and then to pull the national mind this way with Republican statistics to-day and that way with Democratic statistics to-morrow is about as intelligent as to develop a Baptist chemistry and a Presbyterian physics. To put politics on a fact-basis may well play havoc with the traditional tactics of our parties, but, if the choice must be made, intelligence must fight for the party of fact rather than the fact of party. Politics should be the point at which knowledge meets life and becomes socially effective. The art of high government consists in bringing knowledge and power into a working partnership. And it is not safe, as Dean Inge suggested some years ago, to go on indefinitely with the theory of government in the hands of experts who have knowledge, but no power, and the practice of government in the hands of politicians who have power, but no knowledge.

The case for expertness in modern government is clear, but the effective relating of expertness to the processes of democracy is easier said than done. The expert is never the idol of the crowd. The majority is inherently jealous of the minority man who possesses a specialized superiority. It does not willingly elevate him to a position of power over its affairs. As Plato suggested long ago, the crowd in a democracy tends to turn the logic of government upside down and convert leaders into followers and followers into leaders. This unpopularity of the expert with the crowd has delayed the full, effective, and permanent use of expertness in American government. This is why expertness in relation to the formulation of policy, save on the level of routine, has been left to the incidental recruiting of unofficial or quasi-official advisers to serve temporarily in this or that administration.

But, assuming that events have proved more compelling than the envy of the crowd and the case for expertness in government has been proved beyond resistance, the problem remains of fixing the function of the expert in government and of making permanent provision for his proper correlation with legislative and executive leadership. Realism is important at this point. The expert can play havoc with government unless the limitations of specialized judgment are taken into account and the specialist restricted to functions for which the temper and technique of specialization fit him.

The expert is little more likely than the layman to possess dependability of judgment outside his specialism. Even the most distinguished scientist will often bring a strangely unscientific quality of mind to affairs outside his own field.

I have listened to a great scientist describe the progress of his experiments in quest of the cause and cure of a dread disease, watching with fascinated intensity the operation of his mind as it worked its way through the tangled elements of his problem, its flawless precision, its ruthless discarding of the irrelevant, its clairvoyant sensing of the significant, its delicate balance that cheated no factor of its rightful weight in the framing of a judgment. And then a month later I have heard this same scientist discuss a political situation. I could hardly believe my ears. All that had made this scientist's mind great, when he was dealing with a scientific problem, dropped from him like a disintegrated garment, when he undertook to deal with a social problem. His precision gave way to passion, prejudice, and partisanship. He reveled in irrelevancies. He walked blindly past the obviously significant. He seemed devoid of any careful sense of justice in weighing the factors involved in the political situation in question. A realist in the dissection of a guinea pig, he turned sentimentalist in the discussion of a government.

It is pertinent to recall what Voltaire said about the ancient Arabian belief, entertained by the lettered as well as the unlettered, that when a half moon hung in the sky the other half was in Mohammed's sleeve. "This Arab," said Voltaire, "who will be a good calculator, a learned chemist, an exact astronomer, will believe nevertheless that Mohammed put half the moon in his sleeve." This ancient Arabian duality of mind still exists in the modern expert who, responsible inside his specialism and irresponsible outside it, lands government in all sorts of futile ventures whenever statesmanship, expecting too much of the expert, trusts him to formulate large policies.

The expert is essentially a specialist in means, not ends. The very intensity of his focus tends to distort his sense of proportion when he undertakes to deal with a problem of political or economic policy upon which a bewildering medley of human interests converge. Effective government in the midst of modern complexity is, I repeat, impossible apart from the service of the specialist. The specialist is not, however, a substitute for the statesman. The statesman is an artist in ends, as the expert is a specialist in means. The function of the expert is that of hewer of wood and drawer of water to the statesman as, with infinite patience and a supreme sense of social needs, social values, and social possibilities, the statesman builds the broad policies that will serve and satisfy the time and the people he is called to rule.

The Roosevelt regime had hardly got under way before a critical storm began swirling about the brain trust it had brought in its train. The more traditional elements in the Democratic party have silently cheered the Republican attack on this thundering herd of experts that suddenly invaded

Washington. Objection to the brain trust stems from two sources. In the first place, the personnel of the brain trust is disliked by the objectors. And, in the second place, the principle of selection rather than election that brought the brain trusters into positions of power is disliked by the objectors.

I am not interested in venturing a judgment upon any individual brain truster the presidential dragnet has drawn to Washington. I know a good many of the men who have fashioned this or that phase of the New Deal. Some of them rise to the stature of statesmen. Some of them are, I think, of doubtful dependability as guides in the difficult process of political, social, and economic readjustment facing the nation. But this mixture of good and not so good prevails in all cabinets and improvised coteries that surround presidents and premiers. If the ratio of good to not so good in the Rooseveltian brain trust is higher or lower than usual, that is an accident of the personal judgment that selected them, and does not spring from any basic philosophy of government.

I am keenly interested, however, in the attack on the practice of using selected men for tasks that elected men have traditionally been supposed to do. The attack is, I am sure, badly conceived and blindly waged. The elective process of democracy does not, by and large, throw up the expert intelligence and specialized background needed for the technical diagnosis and treatment of the political, social, and economic diseases that afflict our social

[60]

order. This failure of democracy to recruit by election a requisite competence has elsewhere led to dictatorship. If it is not to lead to dictatorship in the United States, a wider and wider use must be made of men selected because of particular competence for dealing with particular problems.

The brain-trust idea began with big business. The whole elaborate application of the results of research in the physical sciences to industrial production, that gave us this age of plenty which we have still to learn how to manage, was made possible by the innumerable brain trusts assembled by industrial leadership and installed in the laboratories of American industries. But research in the social sciences did not keep pace with research in the physical sciences, at least at the point of practical application, with the result that the age of plenty these brain trusts of business helped to create got seriously out of hand. It is surely not radical to assume that brain trusts of social scientists might prove quite as helpful in the development of distributive policies as the brain trusts of physical scientists have proved in the devising of productive processes. It surely cannot be safely assumed that, while the creation of abundance calls for expertness, the use of abundance can be left to amateurism.

Government will do well, however, to tear a leaf from the experience of business in the use of experts. Business has blundered at many points, but, in the matter of actually creating an age of plenty on the

[61]

heels of centuries of scarcity, it has succeeded brilliantly. In the field of production, it has contrived to get the best out of its brain trusts. And part of its success in so doing has been, I think, that it has not expected too much from the expert. It has looked to the expert for the raw materials out of which decisions might be fashioned and policies built, but it has left the making of decisions and the molding of policies to business leadership which is to economic administration what statesmanship is to political administration.

Business keeps its brain trusts in the laboratory. Government too often makes the mistake of asking its experts to function in the laboratory and to serve at the executive desk all at the same time. When this policy is pursued, government suffers all the sins and is served by few of the virtues of expertness.

Nothing I have here said is meant to imply that the specialist never rises to the stature of the statesman. He may. Now and then he does. And when the expert escapes imprisonment in his specialism, sees the implications of his field for other fields, deals intelligently with the impact of forces from other fields upon the forces in his field, and contrives to transfer to the field of public policy the scientific objectivity he has brought to his own specialism, he becomes a rare and precious asset of government. But, in such instances, I suspect that the breadth of the expert's judgment is due less to the fact of his

[62]

expertness in his special field than to the fact that natively he is of the caliber of the statesman.

In the fourth place, we should, I think, make specific provision for the adequate training of able public servants. Even the wisest legislation may come a cropper if its translation into action is left to the inept and the amateur. An adequately trained personnel for both a political civil service and an economic civil service becomes increasingly important as the role of the modern state expands.

Government functions on three major levels: (1) the level of policy, (2) the level of administration, and (3) the level of technical operation. The highest achievable training is important at all three levels, but it is at the second level that the current situation calls most loudly for a deliberately devised new training program.

The officers of government who, as legislators and executives, determine the major lines of policy are recruited by processes of popular election and political appointment which are but indirectly influenced by consideration of a special training of the candidate for the special task in question. And while it may be alluring to speculate about government under which state legislators, governors, officers of state, congressmen, and even presidents would be obliged to give evidence of specific training for these posts before entry in any elective race, we know that, as a practical matter, no such policy is likely to prevail within predictable time. And it may be doubted that this field, which

[63]

may be broadly described as the statesman's field, should be subjected to the tight formalizations to which any system of training requirements tends. At this level of government service, we are dealing with the art of politics. And, in this art, an unschooled Lincoln may put the supremest savant to shame. For enrichment of the quality of government service at this first level, the most we can do, perhaps, is to play for a general improvement of the capacity of the crowd to know a good man when it sees one.

Modern government can get its accounting, its statistical compilations, its narrower and more technical economic analyses, and its vast mass of operating routine done effectively without setting up any elaborate training program beyond the existing programs of the schools, colleges, and universities of the nation. We are annually graduating an ample supply of men and women adequately fitted to maintain the necessary government service at this third level. It is true, of course, that the problems with which these third-level services deal in government have special aspects the same problems would not have in private enterprise. But, in some measure at least, these distinctions are taken into account in the normal training the schools, colleges, and universities give in these fields.

It is at the second level of government service, the level of administration, that the major weakness of modern government shows up. As the prob-

[64]

lems of government increase in number and complexity, and as the role of the state expands, more and more of the decisions that really determine the quality of government are made at this level. A growing number of the most vital affairs of government are now dominated, not by the ministers of cabinets, to which we may, if we will, draw the most distinguished capacity the country affords, but by the directors, secretaries, and line officers of a bewildering array of governmental agencies, such as boards, commissions, bureaus, and corporations, which modern governments tend so lushly to improvise. As the influence of these administrators grows, it becomes increasingly important that, in basic capacity and broad training, they be more statesmen than technical operators.

In the United States, we lack, I think, any adequate provision for the particular sort of training that would best fit men for service at this critically important level of administration. In common with a group of my colleagues at the University of Wisconsin, I have been deeply interested to explore possible ways and means of preparing and providing such training, without undue expense to government, and without creating any single West Point of politics as a new institution. To sharpen to a point the plea I have made for a better training for administrative service in government, I may summarize the major conclusions of this group, although various members of the group may not agree with all the distinctions here drawn and all the shadings of emphasis here given to the discussion of the problem.

This Wisconsin group believes that these administrative servants of government need a training broader than the vocationalized expertness of specialized studies alone affords and better integrated than the miscellaneous hit-and-run studies of too freely elective curricula provide. It believes that expert knowledge of the specific problems of economics and statecraft can most surely be brought to life in productive application by administrators who are trained also to a broad and philosophic appreciation of the problems involved in the structure and functions of human society. It believes that the business of administration in modern government can best be discharged by servants equipped with a wide historical perspective, and a sense of how the forces of social causation have operated over the ages, together with an understanding of the more immediate factors instigative of contemporary movements in popular thought and political action. It believes that men in position so profoundly to affect the nature and course of the national life, as these administrators are, should know, from an understanding grasp of history, why and how the basic patterns of social behavior and social control have here stayed firm and there shifted freely through the centuries. Otherwise government is open to the folly of repeating mistakes that have been made again and again in historic experience. It believes also that directors of government should know the soils in which current impulses are rooted. Otherwise government is open to the temptation recklessly to improvise policy without responsible reference to current realities.

Out of a series of separate studies and a sustained run of conferences, this group has projected a schedule of seven years of training for public administration. It includes four undergraduate years, devoted to the development of a basic understanding of the broad processes of government and enterprise, historic and contemporary, two additional years, devoted to a more intensive study of special problems of economics and politics, and a final year, devoted to study, observation, and active apprenticeship in appropriate departments of the federal government.

The curricular content and teaching procedure elaborated by this group might evoke legitimate differences of judgment. I am not concerned to discuss these educational details here. I am interested only to emphasize what seems to me the sound and centrally important contention of the scheme, namely, that the stability and significance of the national future depend upon a more consciously and carefully devised provision of a training, at once cultural and technical, for the men and women to whom we must turn for statesmanship, diplomacy, and the active administering of our increasingly complex enterprise of government.

I should like, in passing, to make only one observation on the educational concept underlying the four undergraduate years of this scheme. It rests upon the, to me, sound assumption that the traditional liberal arts program, with the excessive diffusion and enervating thinness its undue elective freedom has induced, does not and will not produce the solid grounding in historic experience and comprehensive grasp of contemporary affairs requisite to the dependable guidance of government in this modern phase. The excessive departmentalism that has done so much for the advance of technical scholarship must be set aside in any scheme that seeks a creative advance in the social education of the servants of government. For the effective doing of this particular job, it is necessary to turn aside from the meticulous truck-farming of tiny plots of knowledge, and to tackle in some new and more integrated fashion the problem of understanding the age we must govern, its historic impetus, and its future implications.

It may be doubted that the critical need for a new and more nearly adequate training for public administration could be met by the governmental creation of a series of graduate schools of politics devoted exclusively to this task. Even the best of the pioneer attacks the universities have made upon this problem at the graduate level have proved inadequate, for the reason that the training of the graduate years has had to build upon an undergraduate foundation with the inherent weaknesses I have indicated. An adequate training program must reach with coherence and completeness from the beginning of the college years through the years of graduate study and apprenticeship.

I have discussed at some length four basic revisions of democratic procedure looking toward a technique for dealing with crises, a reallocation of functions between the legislature and the executive, the effective relation of expertness to the normal processes of government, and the provision of adequate training for public service. These and like revisions of democratic procedure are important parts of the price we must pay for the avoidance of conditions that have elsewhere led to the destruction of democratic self-government.

It remains only for me to say that, important as these revisions are, they are not, in themselves, guaranty of the survival of democracy in the modern world. I revert to the contention with which I began. The destiny of democracy in the United States will depend, finally, upon our success or failure in solving the economic problem. The liberal republic, as Lucien Romier suggests, is at once the most agreeable and the most fragile of all regimes. It cannot survive social and economic instability. And this dependence upon social and economic stability increases when the liberal republic, as with us, takes on more and more of the character of a direct democracy. Not even Americans will permanently adhere to the democratic philosophy through the momentum of their tradition. Men's loyalty to any form of government depends, finally, upon what it does or fails to do to light and to liberate their lives.

[69]

III

FREEDOM INVADED

THROUGHOUT the Western world all sorts of new controls are closing in on the old freedoms as varied governments announce their determination to plan the life and enterprise of their peoples.

Some of the old freedoms, now frankly renounced by the new politics of planning, never existed save in the formal creeds of politics and economics. The substance of other of the old freedoms long since disappeared, leaving only their shadows to remind us they once were ours, as the shadow of freedom of contract remains when the substance of equal bargaining power is well out of reach. Freedom is neither automatically insured nor automatically destroyed by the fact of a political form. Poverty may regiment the lives of men quite as effectively as any rule of arbitrary power. And inequity may prove quite as destructive of liberty as any tyranny. We have known poverty and suffered inequity in our regimes of extensive freedom.

As long, however, as an unquestioned philosophy of freedom was on the books as our official doctrine, we could comfort ourselves with the thought that, if liberty had here and there lapsed into slavery, it was after all our own fault, that the power to determine our own destiny was after all in our own hands, and that, some day when we got around to it, we would conquer poverty, erase inequity, and invest our political liberties with social reality.

But now the trend of Western politics is away from a philosophy of freedom. A new politics of regimentation lifts its voice articulate and without apology. Moscow may have led the parade with its utter break from the era of private enterprise and political liberty, but, for those peoples who find themselves facing the possibility of less radical but none the less real breaks with the old politics of freedom, Mussolinian Rome has instigated, interpreted, and implemented this trend from freedom in the manner that best illustrates the problem now confronting the Western nations. There is no attempt to conciliate the libertarians. Liberty is set down as the scarlet woman of politics, not the chaste maiden for whom the youth of the early nineteenth century saw fit to die. Order, hierarchy, discipline are offered as alternative ideals to liberty. The principles of the past century are pronounced dead. The political force of democracy is declared spent. "The state," cries Mussolini, "is resuming its right and its prestige as the sole and supreme interpreter of the needs of society." Everything within the state! Nothing without the state! Everything for the state! This is the triple cry of the new politics as expressed

[71]

and exemplified by the New Italy. And what is in blossom in Italy is in bud elsewhere.

Many Americans, noting at least a surface similarity between the early moves of Italian Fascism and the first steps of the American New Deal, not in the seizure of power or any strong-arm suppression of opponents, but in the steady expansion of the role of the state in the life of the people, have begun seriously to ask whether, in the long future, we are to pursue our enterprise in freedom or under regimentation. And this, it seems, is to be the battle-cry of the Republican opposition. On no other issue is there so much confusion of judgment. I want, if I can, to bring some measure of clarification to its mazes.

The one thing common to all the experimental governments of the time, our own included, is a shifting of the balance of power between politics and economics. Alike under the variant leaderships of Stalin, Mussolini, and Roosevelt, the statesman is grasping at reins of power long held by the business man, industrialist, and financier.

In each instance, so far, in which the existing order has been taken in hand by an experimental government, it has been a case of political leadership's stepping in to save a situation that economic leadership had failed to master in any socially satisfactory way. But this is the way the face of history is changed. Emergencies arise. They are met. The situation dictates the action. And then, later, a new philosophy, which may have been

[72]

germinating for a generation in the minds of the theorists, is matured around the action through which the emergency has been met. This has happened before our eyes in the last decade and a half. Post-war capitalism ran amuck. Whether the captains of capitalism were wholly or but partly to blame is beside the point. The debacle darkened and made intolerable the lives of too many people to permit government to stay neutral in the economic confusion and conflict of the time. Some force had to hold the social order together. The state was the obvious force to act in the common interest. And everywhere the state has, in consequence, come more and more into fields before dominated by private interests—in some countries, with radical change in the structure and function of the state; in others, with milder alterations. But everywhere the state takes on new significance. And now, a new philosophy, common to all the experimental governments, is taking shape, a philosophy of statism.

A steady enlargement of the role of the state has, with us, been under way for some time. The impetus to statism cannot be wholly charged to the brain storms of a brain trust. Statism has grown in the United States not so much by the initiative of political theorists as from the pragmatic handling of urgent problems by hard-pressed administrators and upon the actual invitation of industry to government to step into the picture as a partner in the planning of publicly significant economic policies and the control of privately unmanageable economic relations in such industrial fields as oil production, to name one notable instance.

Even under Mr. Hoover the government was intervening in the private enterprise of the people. It rushed to the rescue of banks. It administered restoratives to railroads on the brink of receivership. It became a speculator on the grain exchanges. It propped up tottering manufacturers. It played banker to the farmer. It may have acted more as a brother bringing help than as a boss giving orders, but it was swimming forward in the historic stream leading to statism nevertheless. The fact that Hooverian leadership may have intended to swim back as soon as conditions came to normal does not alter the fact that this historic trend toward statism existed without asking the leave of leadership.

We may, I think, set it down as inescapable that government will play a larger and larger role in the realm of economics whether the White House is occupied by a Roosevelt or a Hoover. The nature of this enlarged role of the state may well be radically different under such widely divergent leaderships, but the fact of its enlargement will, in either case, prove inevitable. The day of a virtually anarchic individualism is dead. And no amount of political rhetoric can revive it. The peculiar circumstances of the power age have made impossible any wholesale reversion of government to the simpler role of a simpler day. The road back is not the way out.

It does not follow, however, that the only choice open to us is between anarchic individualism and an all-embracing state. The problem upon which the genius and judgment of our time should come to focus is the problem of determining wisely the direction and the degree of governmental activity in economic affairs which the new circumstances of an age of science, technology, and power production make necessary alike for the social validity and the economic viability of modern industrialism.

This is the major issue of this generation. That it may be made the football of a purely partisan contest does not detract from its reality. If we do not meet this issue with a deliberate and well-grounded decision, the drift toward statism will be swiftly accelerated. How this acceleration will come about is clear.

In the absence of any clean-cut and comprehensive policy regarding the relation between government and private enterprise, we shall almost surely revert uncritically to an anti-trust legislation which will express an admirable social purpose but embody an obsolete economic conception. I would be the last living American to lift a voice in defense of anti-social monopoly. The necessity for its control is manifest. But the nature of such control is debatable. The method by which we regulate monopoly should help rather than hinder a socially minded economic leadership to

[75]

function with maximum efficiency in this age of large-scale enterprise. It is never necessary to burn down the house to kill the rats.

Loosely conceived legislation in the field of monopoly control may operate to prevent the leadership of private enterprise from bringing to the major fields of production and distribution that measure of large-scale coordination and plan without which a smoothly functioning and socially fruitful economic life is impossible in an age of science, technology, and power production. If, in our legislative efforts to hobble the irresponsibility of private enterprise, we hamstring its strength and unintelligently limit the right of its leadership to lead, we shall but insure the inefficiency of the economic order. And with a continuing, not to say increasing, inefficiency of the economic order, the future can be forecast with measurable certainty.

The old cycles will take on a new severity. We shall have our spurts of speculative prosperity, less frequent in occurrence and shorter in duration, but the effective development of mass production and mass consumption, the two physical starting points of social progress, will be definitely slowed down if not definitively stopped. Popular dissatisfaction with economic arrangements will grow by leaps and bounds. And an unprecedented popular pressure, which it will be unable to resist, will come upon government to run the show. The all-embracing state will have arrived.

This has happened, again and again, elsewhere in the West during the last decade and a half. It can happen in the United States if we fail to deal decisively and in a flexibly intelligent fashion with this central issue of the relation of government to private enterprise under modern circumstances. To bring no opposition to the philosophy of the all-embracing state is to risk its ascendancy by default. Blindly to oppose any expansion of the role of the state beyond the simple police role it played in the early era of small, simple, and slow enterprise is equally conducive to the quick advance of statism.

The circumstances of the age demand a new relationship between government and private enterprise. Otherwise the major part of the political world would not now be struggling to find the foundations for such new relationship. There is more behind the current phase of experimentalism than the hysteria of the herd and the ambition of adventurers. The very efficiency of private enterprise has evolved a productive capacity so vast that private enterprise is dependent as never before upon the economic fortune of the masses. The masses must be well-heeled or modern industry must pull in its horns. It is at this point that the concern of private enterprise and the concern of government coincide.

Some measure of statism is not only inevitable but desirable. If we drift, we shall go too far. If we stupidly set ourselves against historic neces-

sity, we shall invoke a reaction against our blindness that will make us puppets of the state. The
delicacy of the decision at stake in our determination of the relation that shall exist between government and private enterprise cannot be over-
emphasized. I set it down as my considered
judgment that at no point in the imperative
readjustment of our old policies to our new problems is there greater danger of committing national
suicide than in our attempt to determine what is
valid and what is vicious in the current trend
toward statism.

Oswald Spengler, in his *Hour of Decision*, insists
that this whole crushing depression is a direct
result of the decline of state power. When economics dethroned politics, so Spengler thinks,
the seeds of the present depression were sown.
Communism agrees. Fascism agrees. There are
inklings to indicate that some Americans agree.
The answer is not, in my judgment, so simple.

We should think twice before following the lead
of either Italy or Russia with their variant versions
of the philosophy of *The State above All*. Our
system of laissez faire economics has manifestly
run amuck. Order must obviously be substituted
for the anarchy that has too often prevailed in
much of our enterprise. Greater foresight must be
injected alike into the planning of production and
the planning of consumption. But the easiest, the
simplest, and the laziest thing to do is to run to
the government for salvation. That may work well

for a time if the luck of events shoves a strong man to the center of the political stage, as it has in Italy and in Russia. And, in the United States, the fates have certainly captained the state with a man of sincere and socially minded impulses. *note—* But, frankly, I am not sure that we are ready to make even Roosevelt receiver for economic America.

The situation cannot be met, however, with apoplectic appeals to the Constitution and tub-thumping harangues about an individualism that has landed so many individuals in the bread line. The rank and file of Americans believe in rugged individualism, as profoundly as did the pioneers, but they have had their fill of ruthless individualism. Unless I fail utterly to understand their mood, they will drive from power and destroy any leadership that seeks, through a theoretical politics, to impose unnecessary and unworkable restrictions upon the free exercise of a rugged individualism, but, if no other choice is open to them, they will submit to drastic limitations upon their freedom of enterprise before they will knowingly hand themselves back into the power of a ruthless individualism of business, industry, and finance.

I do not mean to suggest that the problem is primarily a problem of the goodness or badness of the leaders of private enterprise. The problem confronting us is not the simple aftermath of a shortage of honesty in business. We have, let us admit, seen the standards of some drop, under the lure of lush profits, to varying levels of dishonesty within the law. And, as will be true to the end of time, a few trusted leaders have betrayed our trust. But this is not the major problem the economic order presents just now. It is not that all the men in Wall Street are sinners and all the men on Main Street saints, as some simple minds, in the fervor of campaigns, seem to believe. It is a question of finding the correlations and fixing the controls that will bring our economic organization into consonance with the circumstances and enable it to meet the requirements of an age of science, technology, and power production.

Some measure of social control of private enterprise has long been imperative. The nature of this control is debatable. Its necessity, in my judgment, is not. We have reached a point in our economic evolution at which some force above the battle of miscellaneous and incoordinate private interests, whether it be the force of self-governing enterprise itself or the power of the state, must insure the adoption, throughout American enterprise, of basic policies respecting wages, hours, prices, profits, and their control devices that will bring our capacity to purchase into such relation to our capacity to produce as will keep American business, industry, and agriculture going concerns ministering effectively to the maximum needs of the millions. Had we been less laggard in developing this social control in the stressless days of prosperity, both the business man and the buying public might have been spared much of the strain that has come upon them since.

It is no longer a question of control or no control. It is now only a question of the nature and extent of the control. This is the battle-ground upon which, in my judgment, both business leadership and the political opposition should take their stand and fight it out. It is quite within the range of possibility to effect a temporary economic recovery without facing this fundamental issue. It is utterly impossible, in my judgment, to do other than stumble shortly thereafter into a still deeper depression, with revolutionary results in the offing, unless now we definitely lay the foundation for a nation-wide application of wage, hour, price, and profit policies that will normally spread the national income widely enough to provide our industrial and agricultural enterprise with an adequate and assured consumer market.

I am under no delusion that this is a simple matter. Many stubborn difficulties must be hurdled in its accomplishment. To determine the policies and control devices that will actually accomplish even a measurable stabilization of the market for a mass-production economy of our sort requires the utmost care and first-hand knowledge of the intricate processes and delicate interactions of business, industry, and finance. When government attempts the task, it begins with obvious handicaps. When it lacks the requisite first-hand knowledge of business, political leadership is likely to

[81]

oversimplify the problem and, by the detailed imposition of like policies upon unlike enterprises, to seal the very source of productive power through which it seeks to accomplish a social good. And American business, industry, and finance have, to date, failed to effect any form of organization through which the more enlightened economic leaders could secure generally throughout American enterprise the adoption of the wage, hour, price, and profit policies and the attendant control devices which they, with their superior insight, have long known were imperative alike for the satisfaction of mass requirements and for the survival of a regime of free capitalism.

It would seem that, for the job of formulating and giving general effect to the basic economic policies here suggested, government has the organization but lacks the knowledge, while private enterprise has the knowledge but lacks the organization. This situation, if left unchanged, will play directly into the hands of the forces making for statism. For, as the need for these policies becomes more manifest through a continued stalling of the economic machine, popular demand will turn inevitably to the seat of readily available power for the achievement of its desires.

In short, if we do not decide, with promptitude and intelligence, what the relation between government and private enterprise is to be in the quarter century ahead, the drift of events will decide it for us.

I am as reluctant as any living American to see the ebullient spirit of private enterprise put in chains to the quality of intelligence that American politics seems able normally to recruit. I am not at all enamored of the prospect of having my own and the nation's life ordered about by bureaucrats. I do not believe that the complex economic life of the United States can ever be run effectively from Washington. I doubt the wisdom and workability of having political persons dictate in detail the risks and routines of American business and industry. And this doubt survives even the gross mismanagement so many leaders of business, industry, and finance brought to the nation's enterprise in the decade before 1929.

There is a priceless value at the heart of private initiative that we must preserve at all costs. This value is now gravely endangered by the whirl of affairs in Washington and the other world capitals where experimental governments are in search of the formulas for a new social equilibrium. This value can find permanent preservation only through the clear thought and constructive action of the leaders of private enterprise.

This is not a partisan fling at Mr. Roosevelt. I am, I hope, a realist. And I set it down as a considered judgment, forced upon me by a sustained study of the passing show, that, if the freedom of private initiative in the United States dies in the next ten years, its friends will have been responsible for its death for having failed effectively to

[83]

modernize its operation in the last ten years. It must be plain by now that, in the decade before the depression, private initiative on this continent was doing its blind best to commit suicide. Under such circumstances, the more a statesman believed in private initiative, the more he would be moved to grab it by the collar and seek to discipline it before it took the last fatal leap. Confronted by a mis-application so tragic in social consequence, neither an intelligent president nor an impatient people will stand idly by and see a whole civilization sink just in order to preserve, in the textbooks and for the use of after-dinner speakers, the dogma of private initiative.

I am profoundly skeptical of many of the mutually contradictory mechanisms of the New Deal. There is, it seems to me, a rather heavy strain of Alice in Wonderland economics in much of its program. In particular, I think the New Deal, despite its protestations to the contrary, is playing fast and loose with the values of private initiative, permitting the sins of some of its practitioners to obscure the productive virtues of the principle itself. But I am quite as convinced as any New Dealer that some factor of integration had and has to come into the picture if private initiative is to be saved for itself and for its service to the nation.

For myself, I should prefer to see this factor of integration provided by private enterprise itself. And if the leadership of business, industry, and finance will come to bat with a willingness to face the new problems of this new age of science, technology, and power production with a socially responsible program that will prevent the ruthlessness and protect the ruggedness of individualism, no political leadership on earth can win the suffrage of the American people for a program that smacks either of Fascism or of Communism.

The vast majority of Americans are not interested in political or economic theory. They are interested in the practical impact of government and private enterprise upon their lives. As long as the impact is agreeable, they are inclined to let well enough alone. There was no popular clamor for a new deal under the ultra-conservative Coolidge regime. This was not because the masses had any profound interest in the political or economic philosophy of Mr. Coolidge. It was because, in those boom days, the impact of government and private enterprise upon the lives of the voting majority was agreeable. It was only when the basic business of getting food, clothing, and shelter for their families became difficult that millions of Americans turned a ready ear to radical reconsiderations.

I do not cheer this indifference of the majority to the theoretical consideration of politics and social organization. Maybe a more mature people would act otherwise. The fact is we do not. And I set down this fact in confirmation of my conviction that it lies with the leadership of American business, industry, and finance to say how far infringements on private initiative shall permanently go in the readjustments imperatively before us. Nearly everybody in America prefers private initiative, if it will only deliver the goods, but it must be made to deliver the goods in a manner satisfactory to the majority. If the leadership of private enterprise cannot turn the trick, the masses will insist that the state try its hand at the job.

There is a growing school of thought that insists private profit and public service cannot be reconciled. I think they can. They could not in Adam Smith's day. His doctrine that public needs are best served by intelligent self-interest was premature. It was not true then. It did not become true until the economy of science, technology, and power production, with its mass output, came of age. It is true now. And for the simple reason that the adequacy and security of the profits of industrialists can be realized in a mass production age only as industry builds ample buying power and ample leisure among the consuming millions. We have seen unintelligent self-interest land modern industrialists in bankruptcy.

I would that I were gifted with powers of persuasion that would assuredly convince the business men, industrialists, and financiers of the United States that it lies wholly with them to say whether America shall be caught in the sweep of the current trend toward statism with its Fascist right and its Communist left.

Meanwhile the line of soundest policy respecting the relation of government to private enterprise seems to me clearly indicated. Governmental intervention in business processes is often inept. Governmental inspiration of broad economic policy, and, if necessary, its imposition, may now and then be imperative. It is so now. And if government will keep clear the distinction between the broad guidance of economic policy and the detailed regimentation of business, granted an adequate and intelligent response from the leadership of private enterprise, the United States has, I think, the chance to evolve a sounder relation between politics and economics than either the Communism or Fascism of the hour can possibly achieve.

IV

PLENTY RENOUNCED

IT HAS been the essence of the American spirit
to face the future with high expectancy of new
and vibrant possibilities. The American has
been a man of faith. With nothing of the fatalist
about him, and believing profoundly in the invin-
cibility of intelligence, he has always scorned the
suggestion of surrender in the face of difficult
circumstances. He needs to remember and to rely
upon that spirit now. He is confronted by circumstances of extraordinary difficulty which require
decisions more determinative of his destiny than
any he has yet made.

His creative genius invented and set going vast
mechanisms of science, technology, and power.
These mechanisms, it seemed, had solved the
problem of the production of abundance. Through
their wider and wiser use, he had envisioned the
emancipation of himself and his fellows from the
age-old tyrannies of poverty, drudgery, and insecurity. And then suddenly, as if some devilish
witchcraft had jammed their gears, these mechanisms of hope refused to run with the smooth
swiftness that had before marked their operation.

[88]

The depression was on. A new skepticism of this new order of science, technology, and power arose. Might not this new order of enterprise emaciate rather than emancipate mankind!

The American has been dazed by this collapse of his dreams. He is not yet sure whether this is the end of his world or only a phase of purgation, after which, with a cleansed economic system, he can begin again the conquest of humanism through technology. And, in the midst of his confusion, a thousand and one voices are whispering to him that his only hope of salvation and security lies in a deliberate retreat from this age of plenty and a planned return to an age of scarcity.

It is important, I think, that the soundness of this whispered advice be challenged with an unhesitating precision of attack. If this advice is permitted to pass unchallenged into national policy, the deadly nightshade of a new fatalism will cover America, and a healthy growth will not again spring from its soil for a generation to come.

The danger that this advice may be followed is all the more grave because, until now, our attention has been so completely concentrated on the perfecting of a process of production that we have grossly neglected the perfecting of an economics of use upon which an adequate and assured outlet for the output of our productive capacity must depend. The arrest that has fallen upon our enterprise is the revenge reality has taken upon us for this negligence.

[89]

For the better part of a generation, we have been working in terms of an age of plenty, but thinking in terms of an age of scarcity. Our enterprise has been new. Our economics has been old. The transient prosperity of the twenties threw the mantle of a bright delusion over this dangerous maladjustment between our enterprise and our economics. But events are rapidly joining the issue. We shall have to decide, without undue delay, whether we are to explore further the possibilities of this age of plenty or execute a return to an age of scarcity. We cannot go on indefinitely with our enterprise in one age and our economics in another. We must either shove our enterprise back to our economics or bring our economics abreast of our enterprise.

There is more than the profits of the industrialists at stake in this issue. The social stability of the American future is involved.

If the toiling millions can be convinced that greater happiness can be found by declaring a moratorium on scientific progress, throwing the brakes on technological advance, declining to use to the full the vast resources of modern power, and deliberately reducing the enterprise of the nation to simpler and more easily manageable dimensions, well and good. If that is what they want! But that is not what they want. They hunger to have full human advantage of the utmost this age of science, technology, and power production is equipped to bring them in comfort, convenience, and liberation of spirit.

The fact that this hunger has access to political power at a time when the production of abundance is so plainly possible gives it a significance it might not have if this hunger were voteless and these vast mechanisms of science, technology, and power had never been invented. In an age of scarcity, the poor will endure their lot without undue whimpering, but want will not forever stay docile in the presence of potential plenty kept just beyond its reach by manifest failures in social management. Particularly if want may work its will through its political power!

This is why the issue of an economics of plenty versus an economics of scarcity is more than an academic question. The social stability of the American future is, I repeat, at stake in the choice we make between these alternative economies. This is the issue that cuts under all the other issues that crowd the headlines. The utmost clarity of understanding, by both economic leadership and political leadership, of what is involved in this issue is critically important.

In the pioneer phase of the power age, economic leadership underestimated the importance of an economics of consumption. It became almost exclusively absorbed in its development of a technology of production. It brought expertness extraordinary to this development. It ushered us, with amazing speed, into an age of plenty. And then the inevitable happened. Our capacity to purchase did not keep pace with our capacity to produce. We had learned to make things faster than we had learned to use them. Sales slumped. The profits of industry hit a downward spiral. Economic leadership had to pay the penalty for its neglect of economic policy.

At this point political leadership was forced into the picture by popular pressure. Affairs had drifted to a point at which, if national collapse was to be avoided, political leadership had to assume the responsibility for coaching if not controlling the capitalistic industrialism of the United States. There were intelligence enough and vision enough in the ranks of American business men, industrialists, and financiers to prevent the depression or, once it had been permitted, to pull the nation back from the brink of bankruptcy. But it profits a nation little that such intelligence and vision exist unless they grasp the helm and steer the ship into safe lanes. And the best genius of American economic leadership lay mute and inoperative while the nation, at the moment of its greatest promise, fell into the gravest plight of its history.

The time had come when some leadership had to begin the deliberate reconsideration and revision of our economic policies on a national scale if this magnificent technology of production we had developed was not to lie unused, the broken and bankrupt instrument of a people intelligent enough to invent it but not intelligent enough to use it for human emancipation. And let us be honest! As the crisis deepened, there seemed little likelihood that we would find in the ranks of business, industry, and finance a leadership that could and would, on its own initiative and with the requisite promptitude and scope, effect the basic readjustments of economic policy necessary to break the impasse to which the forces of science, technology, and power, in stubborn conflict with obsolete political and economic policies, had brought the American social order. Political leadership had to step into the breach.

The danger now is that, in this maturer phase of the power age, political leadership will underestimate the importance of the technology of production, as economic leadership, in the pioneer phase of the power age, underestimated the importance of the economics of consumption. And it is by no means certain that economic leadership has learned its lesson. The thunderous applause with which business assemblies now greet attacks on current governmental attempts to restrict production may not always be proof positive that those who cheer are ready to join in the creation and application of an economics of consumption that will make any wholesale restriction of production unnecessary.

There are only two choices now open to us. We can, as I have suggested, declare a moratorium on scientific progress, throw the brakes on technological advance, decline to use to the full the vast resources of modern power, and deliberately scale our enterprise down to more easily manageable dimensions. Or we can put our brains to the business of making such readjustments in our political, social, and economic policies as will enable us to take full human advantage of this age of science, technology, and power production. We can rest content with an economics of scarcity or accept the challenge to construct an economics of plenty. The first choice is unworthy of the American tradition. The second choice would mean that the spirit of the pioneers is not dead in us.

To me, the most disturbing fact of the time is the number of Americans, in high position and low, who are falling victim to a defeatist mood, apparently assuming that progress has come to a dead end, that science and technology have been too efficient in producing a limitless output at low prices, and that the thing to do is to plan a lesser output at higher prices.

To restrict production and to raise prices as a general policy is, to me, not liberalism but reaction, not statesmanship but surrender, not creative advance but cowardly retreat. That way lies the subsidizing of inefficiency. That way lies the sabotage of superior management that knows how to bring both the cost of production and the price of products down. That way lies a permanent and perilous lowering of living standards for the swarming millions. It was not for this that the pioneers builded their blood and sacrifice into the foundations of this republic. More goods at lower prices, not fewer goods at higher prices, is the logical goal of an age of science, technology, and power production.

To me, it is incredible that, in a world of tragically unfilled human need, we should now set out upon the Quixotic attempt to increase welfare by destroying wealth or declining to create it. Our ancestors fought valiantly over the centuries to conquer famine. Are we now to say that their conquest has been too decisive? After the sweat and science of generations have brought us out of an economy of scarcity into an economy of plenty, are we to confess that we are incapable of managing plenty, and deliberately legislate modified famine in just those areas of our enterprise where production has proved most efficient? I think history will pass a bitter judgment upon us if, in the midst of such manifest need, we take this road in dealing with the difficulties now confronting our factories and our farms.

I am quite aware that human need is not effective economic demand unless it is equipped with purchasing power. I insist only that it is the first obligation, alike of economic leadership and of political leadership, under an economy of plenty, to refuse to consider reversion even to a modified scarcity until it has exhausted its ingenuity in devising ways and means of translating existing human need into effective economic demand.

I am quite aware that slowing down production, temporarily and at certain points in our enterprise, may now and then prove unavoidable as a transi-

tion measure to regain control of situations that
have got tragically out of hand. When the patient
has fainted at our feet and shows signs of dying, it
is but sense to apply the pulmotor. Breathing must
be restored. That is the first duty. It may be that
the patient has been undernourished and will need
a beefsteak when he is again conscious and sitting
up in bed, but, at the moment, he needs the
pulmotor. The pulmotor will not build him up. It
will save his life. Once he is again breathing and
ready to eat, however, it would be quite as absurd
to try to feed him the pulmotor as it would have
been to have tried to restore his breath with a
beefsteak. The adoption of an economics of scarcity
in an age of plenty, save as a strictly emergency
measure, is an attempt to feed the pulmotor to a
patient who needs a beefsteak.

The immediate economic difficulty confronting
the nation seems to be that, in nourishing the cattle,
we have neglected the patients, with the result
that we have an oversupply of beefsteaks in relation to the number of patients who can pay for
them. And the paramount problem of the time is to
bring the patients into position to buy the beefsteaks they need. Otherwise, if I may thus symbolize the problem of the nation's enterprise as a
whole, the cattle business must reduce its scale.
This plea that we now give as much attention to
the patients as we have given to the cattle is not
radicalism. It is realistic business planning. It is
responsible statesmanship.

If suddenly some vast new market should be discovered, capable of absorbing the existing and potential surplus of our industrial and agricultural production, our worries would be over, the wheels of industry would hum a new national anthem, and the tractors would lumber with ponderous gaiety across our broad acres. Is such a market discoverable? I think it is.

While I take no stock in the new cult of Little Americans who are turning their backs upon the rest of the world, and preaching a doctrine of self-contained nationalism, I am quite aware that no such market is likely to be found abroad in the decade immediately before us. The turmoil of Europe and the East is too disruptive of normal relations and too destructive of financial security to permit anything like a prompt return to a normal flow of exchange in goods and services. World trade is by no means the dead dog the economic nationalists would have us believe, but its nature and its volume have changed profoundly since the war. Its gross volume may again climb to new heights, but, commodity by commodity, the picture will never again be the same. Foreign markets will be of critical but not controlling importance in the immediate future of American enterprise.

We shall find the major clue to the conquest of our difficulties at home. There is a vast new market, an unexploited business Eldorado, in our midst if business and industrial leadership will but see it and set seriously about its creative development.

This unexploited Eldorado of American business and industry is made up of the millions who are to-day too poor to buy beyond the bare subsistence level. Private capitalism's surest guaranty of permanent and prosperous survival lies in the conquest of poverty on this continent.

Let me digress for a moment to define the term poverty as here employed. As I use the term, I do not mean utter destitution. I mean an income insufficient to provide the minimum of goods and services essential to the maintenance of decency, health, and comfort. There is something approaching agreement among the most dependable students of the social situation on the income a standard family of five needs for the maintenance of decency, health, and comfort. This measurably agreed-upon figure is the factor that leads me to the belief that the one potential market which, if opened up and equipped with buying power, would solve our problem of sluggish surplus and industrial slowing down lies in the millions of Americans living at or below the poverty level.

I accept as certainly not excessive the estimate that, in the period from 1919 to 1929, a farm family of five needed an income of approximately $1,800 to keep it above the poverty level, while a city family of five needed an income of approximately $2,000. If we further break the poverty range down into gradations ranging from a level of serious inadequacy and insecurity to a level of minimum subsistence which affords no provision for emergencies or excursions into the realm of extra comfort or cultural engagements, dependable analysis would seem to indicate that, in the period from 1919 to 1929, an income of approximately $1,400 was needed to keep a farm family of five above the lower poverty level, and an income of approximately $1,800 to keep it above the upper poverty level, while an income of approximately $1,500 was needed to keep a city family of five above the lower poverty level, and an income of approximately $2,000 to keep it above the upper poverty level. And I suspect that utterly accurate analysis would indicate that these incomes enabled families to live at rather than above the levels noted.

Since 1929, the situation has grown more rather than less serious for Americans living at the lower income levels. As the depression deepened, income dropped faster than living costs. And under sincere, but not always closely correlated recovery efforts, living costs have risen faster than income.

If we can determine how many American families reached, failed to reach, or exceeded these minimum incomes essential to the maintenance of decency, health, and comfort, we shall gain, I think, an important insight into one of the major factors that stalled and one of the major forces that can start our economic machine. The statistics of income in the United States give us some guidance here.

I am aware of the limitations that surround statistical averages as a basis for either understanding or action. The human picture behind the figures is never quite the statistical picture painted in terms of averages. If fifteen families have an income of $2,000 each and five families have an income of $500 each, the human situation involved is not that of twenty families each living at a $1,625 income level. But modern statistical studies range widely enough in their samplings, and are careful enough in the selection of the instances studied, to wash out much of the sort of unreality suggested by the extreme instance I have just cited. We may, therefore, gain some guidance at least from the statistics of average income in the United States for the period from 1919 to 1929.

Assuming the soundness of the definition of poverty with which I began, and accepting as not excessive the income ranges commonly considered by experts as needed to keep farm and city families of five above the poverty level, how many American families reached the minimum income levels in the period from 1919 to 1929?

If it took from $1,400 to $1,800 to keep a farm family of five above the poverty level, then over 75 per cent of American farm families lived on the poverty level of minimum subsistence, with no provision for emergencies or excursions into the realm of extra comfort or cultural engagements, while more than 50 per cent lived at a level of serious inadequacy and insecurity.

If it took from $1,500 to $2,000 to keep a city family of five above the poverty level, and if we lump the farm population and the city population together, we find all told some 14,000,000 American families living within the upper and lower poverty ranges as the year 1918 drew to a close. Four million of these families were on the upper poverty level. Eight million of these families were barely within hailing distance of the minimum subsistence level. And 2,000,000 of these families realized an income of approximately $1,000.

This was the situation, as the statistical analysis of average incomes indicates, at the beginning of the boom decade that preceded the depression. What was the situation at the end of the boom decade? Taking the picture at its best in 1929, the contrast throws a brighter illumination over the problem confronting business leadership than is likely to come from a consideration of any other set of factors.

The real wages of the country jumped approximately 40 per cent in the decade in question. What effect did this 40 per cent increase in real wages register in the economic status of the 14,000,000 families living within the range of the upper and lower poverty levels at the beginning of the decade? The most dependable estimates to which I have access, checked and rechecked to the limit of my recourse to expert judgment, indicate that perhaps some 4,000,000 of these 14,000,000 families had lifted themselves above the upper poverty level, although far from the level of affluence. These were the 4,000,000 families which, at the beginning

[101]

of the boom decade, were living at the upper poverty level. The 8,000,000 families which, at the beginning of the decade, were just above the lower poverty level improved their economic status to the extent of crawling to the upper poverty level as I have defined it. And the 2,000,000 families which, at the beginning of the decade, earned $1,000 or less, as an annual income, were still, despite the 40 per cent improvement in their real wages, living at the lower poverty level.

All of which means that, in so far as these statistical averages reflect reality, at the height of the prosperity of the boom decade, some 10,000,000 American families, comprising, perhaps, 33 per cent of our population, were in poverty in the sense of being unable or barely able to finance the minimum requirement of subsistence. In the American families now living at these economic levels is to be found the vast unexploited market to the effective development of which business and industrial leadership should bring its highest genius.

I have a rapidly waning confidence in purely political schemes for equipping these millions with buying power. From a purely quantitative consideration, it is, I think, juvenile to assume that, revising our taxing program drastically upward, we can turn the trick by taking money out of one pocket and putting it in another. There is room for drastic change in the incidence of taxation. There is need for a more productive distribution of the national income alike for the serving of social need and the stabilizing of enterprise. But to transform these poverty-bound millions into paying customers calls for something more fundamental than a wider distribution of the national income as we have known it. It calls for a vast extension of the national income. It calls for a speeding up rather than a slowing down of our productive energy.

Nothing but panicky thinking could have given vogue to the notion that, with 14,000,000 American families below the comfort level at the beginning of the boom decade in 1919, with one-third of our population at the poverty level when the prosperity curve reached an all-time high at the end of the decade in 1929, and with perhaps one-half of the American people within the poverty range in 1933, we had reached a point at which our social salvation and economic recovery depended upon throwing the brakes on our productive energy and resting content with a redistribution of the income from a scaled-down enterprise.

This is defeatism pure and simple. This mood of panic and patent-medicine politics must pass. And then we must buckle down to the job of using our productive powers to the full in the interest of a humanly richer civilization.

And, in estimating the potential new market that lies at our door, if it but had the requisite buying power, we must add to the fact that these millions of Americans now at the poverty level are consuming an inadequate quantity the fact that millions of Americans are consuming an inadequate quality and variety of goods and services. A completely realistic analysis of our problem would indicate, I think, that our most serious problem is not surplus but famine. I do not, let me hasten to add, mean quantitative famine. I mean qualitative famine.

I commend to business and industrial leadership Edith Hawley's illuminating volume on *The Economics of Food Consumption* for a vivid dramatization of the reality of this qualitative famine in one major field of production and consumption. People may starve because the amount of their food is too little. They may starve also because the quality of their food is too low. The first sort of famine is quantitative and spectacular. The second sort of famine is qualitative and subtle. Quantitative famine means death to the individual. Qualitative famine means depletion of the national fiber.

As we swung into the uncertainties of last winter, we said that, as a matter of human relief, no American should starve. That is to say, we intended to see to it that no American should die for want of an adequate quantity of food. Suppose we should add to this determination that no American should die for want of an adequate quantity of food the determination that no American should be depleted for want of an adequate quality and variety of food? I venture the prediction that, if economic leadership should wrestle seriously with the social significance of diet, it would find that, in a generation, we could remake the physical foundations of

human America and, in the remaking, absorb every
food surplus that now haunts us, if we really saw
to it that people everywhere were wisely fed.

In the light of manifest human need for a proper
quality and variety of diet, I am persuaded by
realistic studies that have passed over my desk
that we are to-day underproducing rather than
overproducing many foodstuffs. While we dally
with devices for reducing production even of foodstuffs, America suffers from qualitative famine.
And what is true of foodstuffs is true of most of the
output of our enterprise.

A business and industrial leadership that will
take as its job the conquest of poverty and qualitative famine, as I have here defined them, will
open up the biggest new market we have yet
known, solve such problems of surplus as exist,
realize, even on a narrowed profit margin, larger
total profits than it has dared imagine, and make
the industrial giants of yesterday seem dwarfs.

The achievement of these ends requires, as I
have suggested, that we turn our backs decisively
upon any idea of a retreat to an age of scarcity, and
that we deliberately construct an economics of
plenty in consonance with the prolific productivity
of this age of science, technology, and power
production.

For the better part of a generation, as I have
said, we have been working in terms of an age of
plenty, but thinking in terms of an age of scarcity.
Our enterprise has been new, but our economics

has been old. The old economics expressed the nature and served the needs of the old enterprise of the age of scarcity. It never was the science of wealth it pretended to be. It was, in essence, a science of want. It was little more than a manual of the art of playing hide-and-seek with scarcity. But it is beside the point to quarrel with the creators of the old economics. It reflected the age it was designed to serve. Our concern must center now on the fact that the old enterprise of the age of scarcity, which gave rise to an economics reflecting it, has been succeeded by the new enterprise of an age of plenty, and that this new enterprise calls for a new economics that shall express its nature accurately and serve its needs effectively.

Our whole scheme of private enterprise and political liberty will go down in disaster if we persist in trying to direct the energies of an age of plenty with the economics of an age of scarcity. Neither the success of private enterprise nor the survival of political liberty will long prove possible in a power age apart from a workable and widely applied economics of plenty.

It should certainly be clear by now that an economics of plenty is the one firm foundation upon which a free capitalism can build, with any hope of a permanently prosperous continuance, in an age of lavish productive powers. I shall not presume to sketch the intimate details of an economics of plenty. These cannot be dependably determined in the publicist's library. They must be hammered out on the anvil of practical experience. They must be fitted with fairness and firsthand knowledge to the wide variety of situations a system of private enterprise presents. But a few of the bases of an economics of plenty have, I think, become indisputably clear in the light alike of logic and the living experience of the last fifteen years. These I may venture to state.

There must be no wholesale restriction of production in an age of potential plenty. We must move ahead under full steam. And, although it may be damned as unrealistic and oversimplified by this business man and that economist, we must move generally and promptly in the direction of higher wages, shorter hours, lower prices, and a narrower profit margin per unit of sale or service. All of this can, I am convinced, mean, not only greater social satisfaction to the masses, but greater total profits to the producers.

I do not speak as a new convert to this contention. In season and out of season, at least since 1919 and down through all the days of our bloated prosperity, I lifted my voice and lent my pen to the proposition that we must ground our enterprise upon higher wages, shorter hours, lower prices, and a narrower profit margin or resign ourselves to the increasing insecurity and ultimate collapse of our high-powered productive system. And from the onset of depression until now I have not wavered in this conviction. In addresses to assemblies of representative leaders of American business, industry, and finance at the very beginning of the depression, in my *Thunder and Dawn*, which I wrote in 1931 as prophecy rather than postmortem judgment, and in testimony before the Finance Committee of the United States Senate in February, 1933, I consistently contended that the survival and success of the American economic order depended upon pulling the throttle of production wide open and effecting a wider distribution of the national income, not through any arbitrary political redistribution of existing wealth, but through a wider spread of the week-to-week and month-to-month income of enterprise by a more statesmanlike and, incidentally, more businesslike administration of wages, hours, prices, and profits. And I submit that the events of the last five years have underwritten the soundness of this contention.

We cannot run an economy of science, technology, and power production in low gear. Its nature is such that it must run at full tilt and play for mass production and mass consumption. Otherwise it can neither serve the masses to the limit of its power nor make profits to the limit of its possibility. It chokes itself with unsalable surpluses if it produces to the limit when the masses lack buying power to absorb its output. And it sinks itself under suicidal overhead costs if it tries to operate at less than its capacity. If our economic policies prevent our system of production from running at full tilt, it is but business sense to change our economic policies.

We cannot stabilize an economy of science, technology, and power production through any artificial elevation of prices that protects high production costs, encourages waste, limits output, and tolerates monopoly. We must give our productive energy its head, and adjust our economic policies to its implications.

The need of the moment and the need of the age, as I have said, is more goods at lower prices. I am quite aware that the depression shoved some prices below the profit-making level, granted existing production costs. Granting existing costs of production! That is the fatal assumption upon which so much of the superficial economic thinking of the time rests. Is it either social wisdom or sound business planning to grant existing production costs? There is relatively no limit to the extent to which American ingenuity can go in cutting production costs. It is short-sighted, to say the least, to jack prices to a point at which managerial genius may go lazy on us.

Recovery would, I am convinced, be further along to-day if we had spent less energy in boosting prices, had centered attention more effectively on boosting incomes, with ample credit, governmentally provided if necessary, for wage-paying enterprises during the transition to normal conditions, and had confronted industry with the naked challenge to cut production costs to a point at which profits would be possible at low prices.

[109]

We cannot afford, in the long run, to subsidize any production cost at a point higher than the lowest point to which our best scientific and managerial genius is able to reduce it. Every dollar shaved from production costs by scientific and managerial genius is a dollar freed for investment, if we prove wise enough so to invest it, in the enrichment of American civilization by raising the standard of physical living and widening the opportunity for cultural development through higher wages, shorter hours, and lower prices. If we stabilize a high-cost system of production and stamp out the possibility of a low-cost system of production, we make modern industry at once socially sterile and financially futile.

We cannot insure the continuous effectiveness of an economy of science, technology, and power production apart from a realistically administered but radically conceived shortening of hours. The technocrats may have indulged in cubistic prophecies of quick doom that were more fancy than fact, but the fact remains that science, technology, and power production are annually enabling us to do more work with fewer workers. The modern industrial order is moving, with the relentless inevitability of a Greek tragedy, toward the manless factory as its goal. This goal, save in isolate instances, will remain a theoretical goal, but the incidence of progress toward it is one of the major facts with which business and industrial leadership must deal. Modern industrialism is not so much labor-saving as it is labor-supplanting. This fact makes a socially disruptive unemployment inevitable only if we refuse to adjust our economic policies to it.

Technological advance is making a shorter and shorter working day and working week inevitable, unless we are willing to let technological unemployment work such havoc as it may in our economic order. A shortening of the hours of labor is not a matter of penalizing industry for the benefit of its workers. It is essential to the achievement of that wider distribution of leisure which, alongside a wider distribution of the national income, is imperative if our economy of science, technology, and power production is to have an adequate and assured market for its vast output.

And, finally, we cannot save from collapse an economy of science, technology, and power production if we cling to the philosophy of wages that arose before the era of power production. We are still thinking of wages in terms of the pre-power age. We are still attempting to determine wages in terms of the number of hours a man spends on a job. It is too late to do that. We have moved into the power age in which, from the strictly economic point of view, the person at work is less significant than the power available for getting the work done.

From 1919 to 1929, in forty representative industries, horsepower capacity increased 50 per cent, while the number of employees increased less than 6 per cent. And, since 1929, even while crisis has been freezing so much of our enterprise, inventive genius has been going without sleep in its feverish effort to find ways and means of doing the world's work with more power and fewer people.

This phenomenon of the rising significance of power and the falling significance of people in the production process has brought us to the point at which, if modern enterprise is to remain actively profitable and retain the confidence of the masses, we must begin to determine wages in terms of the amount of power expended rather than in terms of the amount of time spent in producing goods. This is a revolutionary consideration which neither the business man nor the economist has yet fully analyzed or fully admitted. I do not pretend to see the many difficult practical implications of this shift in wage theory. I am simply convinced of its inevitability. It is, I am sure, one of the unavoidable aspects of an economics of plenty with which economic leadership must increasingly concern itself.

If we are not to take the defeatist road of a drastically reduced production, we shall be obliged to determine wages less and less in terms of what we can contrive to buy the time of workers for and more and more in terms of how much of the gross income of industry must be spread out in salaries and wages in order to create an adequate market for the output of our power economy. The old economics of scarcity thought almost exclusively of the producer's interests, seeming hardly to realize that the consumer's interests needed to be considered at all. The new economics of plenty must be rooted firmly in a sustained concern with the prosperity and leisure of the consumer. This is not only socially desirable from the consumer's point of view, but is the only sure safeguard of the producer's interests in an age of lavish productive power. It is the only trustworthy means of insuring the permanently profitable survival of capitalistic industrialism in a power age.

The new economists may listen with advantage to the old prophet, John Ruskin, across a stretch of nearly three-quarters of a century. " . . . consumption absolute," said Ruskin, "is the end, crown, and perfection of production; and wise consumption is a far more difficult art than wise production. . . . capital which produces nothing but capital is only root producing root; bulb issuing in bulb, never in tulip; seed issuing in seed, never in bread. . . . there are two kinds of production always going on in an active state; one of seed and one of food; or production for the Ground and for the Mouth; both of which are by covetous persons thought to be production for the granary; whereas the function of the granary is but intermediate and conservative, fulfilled in distribution; else it ends in nothing but mildew, and nourishment of rats and worms. . . . the wealth of a nation is only to be estimated by what it consumes. . . . The final object of political economy, therefore, is to get good method of consumption, and great quantity of consumption; in other words, to use everything, and to use it nobly; whether it be substance, service, or service perfecting substance. . . . For as consumption is the end and aim of production, so life is the end and aim of consumption."

Under the stern tutelage of the experience of the last five years, we have begun to catch up with this Ruskinian contention that any leadership which concentrates on production to the exclusion of concern with the consumer is a leadership half-blind. In the midst of so much talk about planning production, we begin to see that the process in most urgent need of planning is not production but consumption. And the planning needed is not so much a planning *of* consumption as a planning *for* consumption.

I have insisted that the success of private enterprise in this power age is impossible apart from the prompt construction of an economics of plenty. I want now briefly to argue that the survival of political liberty will, in like manner, depend upon our devising ways and means of putting the full fruits of science, technology, and power production at the disposal of the masses.

None of the experimental governments now in existence would have risen to power had the leadership of the private enterprise of the last half century proved as expert in the development of an economics of consumption as it proved in the development of a technology of production. Granted universal economic well-being throughout the industrialized world, the political status quo would have remained undisturbed, save in areas where political authority proved unnecessarily stupid in its infringement upon the self-respect of its people. The monarchies would still be monarchies, and the democracies still democracies. It may argue a belly-conscious race, but political reform has, of late, stemmed almost exclusively from an economic concern. The masses begin to think their governments politically inadequate when they begin to feel economically insecure.

Lenin, Stalin, Mussolini, Hitler, Roosevelt, and the whole gallery of political experimentalists have flowered from the soil of insecurity. I suspect that not a single one of these governments would have come to power in a national situation of peace, plenty, and a psychology of security.

The masses are always more eager for security than they are enamored of liberty. Liberty is a cause watched over by select spirits that now and then swing the masses behind them. The masses are never hungry for responsibility. They will sell their liberty at the drop of the hat to any leadership that gives promise of governing them handsomely and walling them about with a sense of security. As harassed individuals will fly to the storm cellar of dogma for refuge from doubts, whole peoples will surrender their liberties in return for a feeling of protection from the storms of economic uncertainty.

No political opposition to political experimentalism will get far by damning it as unconstitutional

[115]

or heresy to this or that American tradition if the masses feel that it is the only program in the field that is even trying to bring security to their lives. In a phase of insecurity like this, the masses, when they come to vote, are more interested in the security of the sons than in the faith of the fathers. Empty stomachs cannot be stirred to a fanatic interest in freedom.

The mass demand for economic security will grow louder and louder. My fear is that the politician will hear it, while the business men, industrialists, and financiers will not. If that happens, we shall be in for a generation of legislation that will level the men and enterprises of the United States down to a slimly secure but uninspiring and, in my judgment, ultimately unproductive life even for the masses. I refuse to believe that we are doomed to the destiny of fairly well-clothed and fairly well-fed helots of a standardized state. And yet it is to just this that political pressure from the masses will drive us unless business and industrial leadership promptly and effectively develops a workable and widely effective economics of consumption.

I want security for all as ardently as any Stalin wants it, but I want it in terms of a civilization that knows how to correlate security and freedom. I want to will to my son an America in which a great economic leadership has boldly recast its economic policies for the distribution of wealth to reflect its technical processes for the production of wealth. In such an America, security for all will not mean ironing the life of the nation down to the drab sameness of a Shaker village. Security for the masses is not incompatible with high adventure and high prizes for exceptional genius which, in all ages, has alone produced the ideas and inventions that have worked to lift mankind above a brutish contentment with warm backs and full bellies.

The business men, industrialists, and financiers of the United States should just now be more ardently reformist than Roosevelt. That way lies their salvation. With their first-hand knowledge, they can, if they will, give us reforms that will save us instead of sink us. But, if industry does not give us an economics of plenty, government will give us a politics of security. Some leadership must somehow attempt to spread a buying power that will give the millions satisfactory access to the plenty we are so obviously equipped to produce.

All of which leads me to the crucial question. How shall we go about bringing our capacity to purchase abreast of our capacity to produce? By what means shall we effect this imperative spread of buying power? And who shall assume responsibility for the spreading? Shall government do it? Or shall private enterprise undertake the job?

The answer here is the same that must now be made to every question respecting economic policies that are essential to the security of the masses and the survival of our social order. If private enterprise will do it, government will not attempt it. If private enterprise will not attempt it, government must try to do it. At every point where some new social control has become imperative, if the leadership of private enterprise will provide that control, government will gladly refrain from seeking it through any regimentation of the nation's life and work. If, on the other hand, the leadership of private enterprise fails to provide that control, government must undertake to provide it. It will have no choice. Any government that refuses to attempt, either through private enterprise or in spite of it, such new controls as may have become imperative will be ruthlessly thrown out of power by a disillusioned and determined people.

If government is left to take the initiative and responsibility for spreading buying power widely enough to save the mechanisms of this age of plenty from collapsing, there are but two ways in which, through positive action, it can go about it. Let me glance at these two ways in passing.

Through what it does respecting the taxation of incomes, corporation activities, excess profits, capital gains, estates, and the like, as well as through the use to which it puts the funds it thus raises, government can go far toward spreading the national income more widely and can, through the exercise of the taxing power, exert a very effective control over economic processes generally. It can stop development on this sector of the industrial front through near-confiscatory taxation, speed up development on that sector through preferential taxation, while it holds things at even keel on another sector through taxation that veers toward neither extreme.

Government can, on the other hand, tackle the problem of spreading buying power through the imposition upon business and industry of revised policies respecting wages, hours, prices, and profits. If it were the possessor of perfect wisdom, government could increase the national income greatly enough and spread it widely enough to give our industrial system a stable consumer market by enforcing upon our total enterprise the policies that the ablest and wisest business leaders have found commercially profitable because they are socially sound. This would be a more delicate and more complicated task than any of the codes yet devised have accomplished. The regulations involved would have to be as varied as the variations of enterprise itself.

Taxation has a legitimate role as an instrument of social control. But it is a limited role. Taxation should not be made the major instrument of social control. We shall have a sounder and surely a more congenial civilization if the necessary distribution of the national income is effected through the day-to-day processes of business and industry, with the working millions getting the available over-plus directly and spending it through normal channels, than if government takes the over-plus and spends it on lavish public works and lushly expanded public services. There is room for a liberal enrichment of many public services of government, but that is something apart from going out of our way to find things upon which government may spend money as a method of spreading buying power.

Buying power must be spread if our economy of science, technology, and power production is not to stay stalled, but I am not a little disturbed by some of the attempts that political leadership is here and there making to reach this manifestly desirable end. Radical statesmen and reactionary captains of industry join hands to cure the depression by planning a lesser output at higher prices. I do not like this amazing merger of radical politics and reactionary economics. And I like even less what radical politics seems bent upon doing at the point where it breaks with reactionary economics. After swallowing whole a program for the control of production, the creation of scarcity, and the fixing of prices which has always been the dream of reactionary economic leadership, a radical politics sets the stage for heavier and heavier taxation of the results of successful enterprise in order that the government may execute lavish public works to which the masses will have access, on the theory that this will effect the spread of buying power which good business judgment indicates and the circumstances of the power age demand.

This, it seems to me, is missing the point. I do not suggest that industrial enterprise, incomes, and inheritances cannot stand heavier impacts of taxation. I insist only that we shall never build a great civilization by lavish expenditure on even the most desirable public works before we have solved the problem of clothing the bodies, filling the stomachs, and freeing from fear the hearts of the masses. And until we do this basic job in and through the nation's business, industry, and agriculture, we shall have evaded rather than solved our problem. The place to solve the economic problem is at the source where policies respecting wages, hours, prices, and profits are formulated and fixed. It is no answer to permit an economic system to play havoc with the lives of millions and then step into the picture with stringent taxes to take care of these millions with the munificence of a political Santa Claus. In the end, such procedure will wreck the system that must produce the wealth and will sap the self-respect of the millions who learn to lean on the bounty of government.

I applaud the willingness of any leadership that goes bravely to bat in a moment of crisis and, without standing on ceremony, does whatever may be necessary to see to it that men and women and children are fed and clothed and sheltered. But relief and economic realism present different problems. Long-time statesmanship requires that we go beyond planless borrowing to bolster up an economic order that does not, in its normal day-to-day operation, spread buying power widely enough to stabilize an adequate market for its output and give to the millions those basic factors of goods, services, and leisure which are the essential raw materials of satisfactory living. And it is, I repeat, in the authentic processes of economic enterprise, not in the artificial processes of political action, that the economic problem must finally be solved.

In phases of crisis, political action is accorded a position out of all proportion to its actual power permanently to benefit the lives of men. The genius of government is essentially regulative. It is not creative. It is more adept with the bit than with the spur. When government undertakes to deal directly with the dynamic forces of modern enterprise, its impulse is to curb. It is tempted to scale the problem down to its capacity for management.

If now we take the road of repression, restriction, and reduction through intimate government supervision, we shall dry up the well-springs of that directive and developmental genius which, whatever its shortcomings in the field of economic policy, has given distinction and drive to American enterprise. The situation suggests, it seems to me, a drastically different approach. Open the throttle! Say to the best business and industrial genius of the nation, "Go ahead. Invent ways and means of making more goods and rendering more services at lower prices. We will not call you criminal if you do. We will reward you, and reward you handsomely. But we will insist that you construct and apply wage, hour, price, and profit policies that will surely build a dependable market for your lush output, lift the standard of living for all classes of

Americans, and make impossible crises more grave than the irreducible minimum of ups and downs that all human enterprise must experience. And, in the end, both you and the masses will be better off. But, bear in mind, if you do not promptly give evidence of such policies, government must take you in hand and, despite its limitations in the field of creative enterprise, try to invest your policies with greater social validity." We must stabilize our enterprise. If private leadership does not, then public leadership must try. But we must draft our plans for stabilization with the utmost care.

There were important values involved in the blind rush of seeming overproduction that played so significant a part in landing us in the slough of depression. We may have overbuilt some of our plants. We may, here and there, have been short-sighted in laying out production schedules that overshot the then available market. We may have let our devotion to free competition land us in a crazy carnival of unplanned production. But there was a vibrant creativeness at the heart of our craziness. Our inventive genius was unleashed. We sat up nights improving our techniques. There is some ground for wonder whether, under a regime of rigid planning, we would have made the amazing headway in production we did make in that riotous era when the sky seemed the limit.

But, for all the good side of that planless phase, the economic house tumbled about our ears. We know now that we must consciously stabilize our

enterprise. We must keep crystal clear, however, the distinction between a true and a false
stabilization.

A false stabilization will simply put a bit in the
teeth of the wild horse of production, slowing down
his pace until he trots amiably along at the same
gait the tamer horse of current consumption is able
to maintain. A true stabilization will not be
content with any such acceptance of current con-
sumptive power as a standard by which to determine production. It is not a static balance between
production and consumption that a true stabilization will seek. The goal of a true stabilization is
simply regularized growth. But *growth*, mind you!
The only valid objective of American industry is
the intelligently regularized use for human benefit
of the maximum possible production. And this
means that the key to any true stabilization of our
enterprises lies in bringing the rate of growth in
purchasing power up to the rate of growth in producing power. It is the small talk of small men to say
that the market, as we know it, should willy-nilly
dictate production.

We must be careful lest our programs of stabilization turn out to have been processes of sterilization.
To play down our productive powers may well
result in a stabilization of want rather than a
stabilization of welfare.

The productive energy we have generated can,
under an economics of plenty, be mankind's hope.
Under an economics of scarcity, it may prove a

hangman's noose. Scientific and technical leadership have abolished the physical necessity of poverty in the United States, in the sense even of the liberal definition of poverty I have adopted in this study. It remains for political and economic leadership to abolish the social fact of poverty and its milder manifestation of underconsumption. All the necessary tools are in our hands for emancipating the race from poverty, drudgery, and insecurity. If now we fail to effect this emancipation, and are content with a procedure of planning that adjusts us to the half-hearted and insecure existence of a politically reinduced age of scarcity, we shall go down in history as traitors to the tools of our own creation.

For these reasons, it is important, I think, that we judge every political leadership bidding for our suffrage and every economic leadership that asks our confidence, whether it comes with the lugubrious warnings of conservatism or the lilting promises of liberalism, by this: Is it proposing bravely to bend to human use the full powers of this economy of science, technology, and power production which our genius has created, or does it ask us to take a coward's refuge in a policy of repressing, restricting, and reducing its maximum productive capacities?

V

SCIENCE BETRAYED

I HAVE been compelled to refer again and again, with a repetition that nothing but necessity could justify, to the impact of science, technology, and power upon the traditional structure and functioning of our social order. In the generation now ending, these three forces of social modernism have enjoyed a vast prestige. To this trinity the modern West had tethered its hope for a progressively higher and more human quality of social existence. But their reputation as saviors has suffered a slump in this phase of disillusionment that depression brought to the Western peoples.

The current plight of the three is summarized in the current status of science in the public mind, for technology and power production are but the fruition and formal application of science to industrial enterprise. An examination of this status is important in any attempt realistically to assess the American outlook, for the relation of science to social management cannot but remain one of the major considerations of modern statesmanship.

The tables have been turned. For a good stretch of years, the scientists have been confronting society with the necessity of difficult readjustments in its procedures. Now society is confronting the scientists with the necessity of difficult readjustments in their procedures. The crisis in society has precipitated a crisis in science.

The physical sciences and the social sciences are alike confronted by a spreading skepticism of their effectiveness as agencies of change and control in modern society. The physical scientists are blamed for having caused the confusion and collapse that have fallen upon so much of Western life. The social scientists are blamed for having failed to prevent this dishevelment of affairs. That these reactions may be oversimplified and emotionalized is beside the point. The reportable fact is that the climate of opinion in which research must be administered has been radically changed since 1929.

This changed climate of opinion in which research must be administered reflects three shifts in the attitude of the public mind toward science: (1) A growing dissatisfaction with the fag ends of an era in which a laissez faire science has thrust into a laissez faire society a bewildering multitude of new facts and new forces that have produced extensive maladjustments and imposed severe strains upon the traditional structures and functions of the political, social, and economic orders; (2) a growing disillusionment with a process of research in which the production of new knowledge has not been accompanied by a more effective effort to prevent its application from causing more troubles than it cures; and (3) a growing determination to have the political, social, and economic developments of the future better planned and better controlled.

These three shifts in attitude have generated a new mood respecting science. This new mood has been reflected in the budgetary policies of state and national governments respecting the support of research and the institutions of education in which science has its formal home. Official support of science has, of late, become uncertain, as even the most hurried survey of federal and state budgets will indicate. And this uncertainty of support has, in striking instances, been greater than the fiscal difficulties of government made necessary. This new reluctance to support science and its cognate enterprise of education cannot be wholly attributed to the normal impulse of a people, when harassed by hard times, to spend money only upon the more immediately obvious necessities.

A digest of the messages of the governors of the several states for the last five years, as these messages have related to reduced support for scientific and educational enterprises, does not, in general, reflect the reluctance and regret such messages would have expressed ten years ago. On the contrary, again and again, schools have been scuttled and science put on a starvation diet less upon grounds of financial stress than upon grounds of dissatisfaction with the social return from the scientific and educational investment to date.

A comparative analysis of the reduced expenditures and the increased expenditures of the Roosevelt regime, for purposes which the existing agencies of science and education are designed to serve, reveals the fact that, for every dollar cut from the support of the traditional scientific and educational agencies of government, several dollars have been provided for improvised agencies to serve the same purposes.

And this new reluctance to support science and education cannot be interpreted as the angry reaction of a visionless riff-raff that is sometimes washed up into positions of political power by the tides of social discontent. Some of the most drastic withdrawals of support from the scientific and educational enterprises of our states have been dictated by university-trained governors, while a drastic disruption of many critically important scientific services of the federal government has been threatened under the auspices of a President with a Harvard degree.

It is possible to put a variety of interpretations on all this. Some may regard it as but a by-product of the phase of panic through which we have been passing. Some may regard it as but the epidemic of unenlightened economy that seems inseparable from phases of financial stringency. Some may regard it as the exertion of an enlightened, even if temporarily disruptive, pressure from the outside for internal readjustments in the programs and processes of the nation's scientific and educational establishments that shall modernize, enrich, and bring to better social focus their contribution to the processes of revaluation and redirection upon which the stability and significance of the national future are so manifestly dependent.

No one of these interpretations alone tells the whole story. Each takes into account some factor that materially affects the current situation. Together they underscore the fact that the crisis in society has precipitated a crisis in science, and that, in consequence, the research of the decade ahead must be determined and directed in the light of a changed social attitude toward science.

I have defined this new mood respecting science as a mood reflecting a growing dissatisfaction with the maladjustments and strains that the results of research have brought to the traditional forms of government and enterprise, a growing disillusionment with a research that does not accompany its production of new knowledge with a more effective effort to direct its application to more uniformly constructive ends, and a growing determination to bring a larger measure of deliberate planning and control to the developments of the future.

It may be said that the dissatisfactions, disillusionments, and determinations reflected in this mood spring from an uncritical resentment against political, social, and economic blunders for which the scientists cannot justly be blamed. It may be said that the sole business of science is to produce new knowledge, and that to clutter its laboratories with considerations of the social implication of their output would but make science less efficient. It may be said that the current passion for planning overestimates the capacity of the race to rule its bewilderingly varied and complex affairs with the foresight and fine attention to detail that less complex and more controllable enterprises permit.

But, whether it be well-founded or ill-founded, this new mood respecting research exists and must be reckoned with by all those concerned with enriching the service of science to society, as an engineer must reckon with the strains that will surely come upon the bridge he has been commissioned to construct. If the implications of these current attitudes toward research are not met, with promptitude and intelligence, it is not impossible that we shall witness a widespread revolt against science and a withering retrogression of the whole educational enterprise.

The prestige of the scientist and the productive utilization of his findings in the decade ahead will, in my judgment, depend upon whether research that is at all related to the broad problem of social management is planned, executed, and interpreted in the light of this triple-based mood which, however wrong in some of its assumptions, is right in its central aim.

This mood will condition the future and fortune of research for a good run of years to come. It is more than a transient whim. It is a mood that grows out of what is, perhaps, the most serious phenomenon of modern times, namely, the race between scientific progress and social instability. Researchers fired the gun that started this race. And those who pulled the trigger cannot wholly escape responsibility for the resultant casualties.

The development of scientific processes has moved with airplane speed. The development of social policies has lagged at a stage-coach rate. The physical sciences have produced social changes faster than the social sciences have perfected social controls. All sorts of maladjustments have occurred. The result has been this race between scientific progress and social instability, with instability, for the time being, in the lead. Many of the governments and business directorates of the time resemble nothing so much as a nervous spinster glaring with frightened eyes through the windshield of a motor gone wild.

A laissez faire science, functioning in a laissez faire society, has seen a ruinous social instability follow in the wake of rapid scientific progress. Down to fairly recent days, the mine run of mankind did not connect the two. An uncritical enthusiasm for science mounted higher and higher despite the bombshells research was pitching into the midst of our traditional processes and policies. But, during the last five years, it has filtered down to growing millions, who may read no more than their daily newspaper, the Sunday supplement, and an occasional magazine, that the revolutionary results of physical science and industrial technology have brought our traditional order of life and enterprise to a historic turn in the road.

Millions of Americans, who have never heard of the social lag, are to-day sensitively aware that social control has not kept pace with social change induced by scientific research. This fact of social lag, which but a little while ago was an esoteric topic among the intelligentsia, is to-day wrestled with by the rank-and-filers in the smoking rooms of any train. The gravest threat in the offing is that this growing sense among the voting millions that scientific progress has got socially out of hand may lead to a ruinous relaxation of interest in and support of science unless ways and means can be found to modulate and humanize the impact of science upon society.

Research has moved countless millions out of the ancient shelters in which they had a decent measure of economic security, social stability, and spiritual peace, even if the life lived there was meager in content and convenience, and has left them unsheltered under the storm-swept skies of a strange world. In this strange new world, born of research, these millions have had a few more gadgets in bathroom and basement and there has been a transient lift in living standards, when the going has been good, but they find even these boons snatched suddenly from them in this current phase of economic insecurity, social instability, and spiritual confusion.

Any scientist who cannot see in all this a situation out of which might come a popular revolt against science and a social throttling of research by a political leadership responsive to crowd whims has lived too long in the subdued light of the cloister to see clearly in the broad daylight of human affairs. And any scientist who does not see in all this an imperative summons to modulate and humanize the impact of modern science upon modern society is something less than the society supporting him has the right to expect him to be.

I set it down, then, as a matter of critical importance to the future of research, in the physical sciences no less than in the social sciences, that scientists should come together in a conscious and common effort so to plan, prosecute, and publish their researches that the scientific progress of the next quarter century shall, as far as may be humanly possible, stabilize and enrich the life of state and nation instead of producing a further and, perhaps, fatal social instability.

This is, I admit, asking scientists to assume a new obligation. Traditionally, scientists, in social as well as in physical research, have been reluctant to assume responsibility beyond the production of new knowledge. They have tended to lift aloofness to the dignity of a virtue, assuming, when they have not asserted, that scientific objectivity is impossible apart from social neutrality. They have built their laboratories on the side-lines of the social turmoil and sound-proofed their libraries from the cries of the street.

This tradition of aloofness has here and there been broken by professors who have become suave brain trusters or swashbuckling campaigners. Such individual variants have not always been the best exemplars of science in the service of society. And this direct sort of participation in social management is not, let me make clear, what I have in mind in this plea for a reconsideration of research in terms of the current social situation.

I am not suggesting that the scientist desert his laboratory and run for office. I am not suggesting that the scholar be forever rushing into print with manifestoes telling business men and politicians how to run their affairs. I am not suggesting that chemists, physicists, geologists, and like men of the laboratory relax the concentration of their energies upon their respective specialisms and squander their time on amateur excursions into political science and economics. I am not suggesting that the creatively anarchic individualism of the pure scientist be tampered with. To the end of time, he should be permitted to follow his own nose when it scents a new and inviting trail into the unknown. I am suggesting only that, aside from those fundamental researches dealing with matters obviously still far from the stage of social implication, research in general should be planned, executed, and interpreted with a living sense of its immediate and long-time impact upon the structure and functions of the society which conditions our lives and enterprises.

I realize that even this suggestion runs counter to two assumptions that have long prevailed in scientific circles. It has been assumed that the production of new knowledge is intrinsically and inevitably good, and that, if a new fact blights instead of blesses mankind, the blame must rest upon predatory business men, blundering politicians, or ignorant individuals who have misapplied the fact, not upon the scientists who have made the fact available. And it has been further assumed that responsibility for considering the social impact of modern science upon modern society is a specialized responsibility resting exclusively upon the social scientists and is no business of the physical scientists.

I submit that events have conclusively shattered the first assumption, and that experience has proved the second assumption inadequate.

If we are concerned to maintain the continuity of modern science, we cannot, in my judgment, longer hold to the aloof assumption that the production of new knowledge is automatically and always good. In the long reach of the centuries this assumption doubtless holds, but mankind, at least in phases of such complexity and stress as this, does not think in centuries. It thinks rather in terms of the next meal or the next election. Even statesmen have difficulty in remembering that the unborn are part of their constituency. It is this none-too-rarefied reaction of the crowd, whose votes in the end dictate the national budget and determine the national being, with which the scientists must finally reckon. For good or for ill, the next quarter century will, unless I am far afield in judgment, see an increasingly close social scrutiny of science by the crowd. And, if the prosecution of research continues to result in a greater and greater social instability, the crowd may drastically reduce its support of research and take steps to control the release and utilization of its results.

It may justifiably be said that any such popularly imposed embargo on the relentless exploration of the unknown would condemn American civilization to the black death of ignorance and result in a barrenness of life more destructive of the human spirit than the current instability. But civilizations have, before in history, taken steps quite as suicidal! Such a secession from the age of science is not impossible if the enterprise of research is kept too severely segregated from its social implications.

When some years ago the Bishop of Ripon seriously suggested a ten-year moratorium on research to give society a digestive pause, a chance to establish effective social control of the new forces released by the research of the preceding decade, we could dismiss the suggestion as the nervous generalization of a cleric who might have had a bad night. We cannot so lightly dismiss the dangers hidden in the hysteria of a generation that has

[137]

seen its civilization run amuck in the midst of its greatest scientific productivity.

The social scientists cannot, in my judgment, rightly be saddled with the sole responsibility for the wise human use of the results of the whole round of scientific research. I have, in fact, a haunting sense of unreality when I speak of the social sciences as a field apart from the physical sciences. As I run my eye over what the physical sciences have done to the lives of men, I am persuaded that physics, chemistry, and bacteriology are quite as social as sociology. There is danger in the distinction we have drawn between the social sciences and the physical sciences. A single responsibility has been split to the point where everybody's business has become nobody's business. Under the existing procedure of the sciences, society is not getting the benefit it might from either the social sciences or the physical sciences.

To date the researches of the physical scientists and the researches of the social scientists have been so segregate that the social scientists have had little more than the layman's knowledge of what the physical scientists were unearthing. And the physical scientists have been quite as insulated from the problems with which the social scientists were wrestling. The results of research in the physical sciences, as these results have been translated into action by the technologists, have been among the most important factors in producing the current phase of social instability, but the men who have produced these results in the first instance have, by and large, given little attention to their ultimate social impact. If their application wrought havoc, that was a problem to take sleep from the pillows of the social scientists! But, as research generally has been organized in these later years, the social scientists have entered the picture too late to do much about it, even if it were socially sound to hold them wholly responsible for the wise use of the results of research in the physical sciences.

It is imperative, I think, that our universities, research institutes, and industrial laboratories organize to insure an earlier consideration of the political, social, and economic effects of the discoveries of the physical scientist and industrial technologist. Under the research system to date, as I have indicated, the social scientists get into the game too late. They wait until the discoveries of the physical scientist and industrial technologist radically upset old social and economic arrangements and then come along as a kind of wrecking crew to clean up after the catastrophe and to suggest ways of preventing its recurrence. That has proved too costly a procedure. We must devise a method of continuous cooperation between the physical scientists and the social scientists in all our research centers. The social scientists must be kept informed of what the physical scientists are up to, not after the physical scientists have worked social and economic havoc with their discoveries, but from the very beginning of their researches.

If the chemists or physicists are on the trail of a new idea in 1934 that may prove workable in 1954, the social scientists should know it in 1934, not in 1954. And, through all the twenty years between 1934 and 1954, the social scientists should be considering ways and means of making this new idea help instead of hamstring humanity if and when it becomes workable.

If we can invent such a method of sustained cooperation between the physical scientists and the social scientists, we can shorten by at least a decade the lag between the swiftly changing processes and the slowly changing policies of our national life.

VI

EDUCATION HAMSTRUNG

ANY assessment of the current American
scene that is dependably to guide us in the
formulation of policy for the future must
take fully into account the status and prospect of
the schools and cognate instruments of special
and mass education to which we must look for the
development of superlative leadership and stably
intelligent followership.

This becomes doubly imperative at the present
juncture to which the forces of science, technology,
and power production have brought the American
order of life and enterprise. The reasons for this
are many and manifest. I mention but two. Alike
in public service and private enterprise the problems with which leadership must now deal are
unprecedentedly complex and call for an unprecedented richness of information, insight, and
intelligence. This fact alone underwrites the necessity for maintaining the highest attainable quality
of education. And to this fact must be added the
fact that, as political leadership moves to eliminate
child labor and as economic leadership moves
toward the doing of the world's work with fewer
and fewer workers in less and less time, the new

freedom of children and the new leisure of adults throw a vast new load upon the national machinery for formal and informal education. The situation, in short, calls for an increased quantity and an intensified quality of education at a time when, unhappily, both the quantity and quality of American education are threatened.

A sword hangs over education throughout the United States. Never before in the United States and nowhere else in the civilized world has a depression been permitted to scuttle the schools and rape the intellectual resources of the national future. The panic of 1837 ended in the renewal, not in the ruin, of the schools. Between 1837 and 1843, leading American states increased their support of education as much as 34 per cent. The panic of 1857 left the schools unharmed. The panic of 1873, despite its severity, did not result in any backward step in education. In twenty-nine representative states, the financial support of the schools was averagely increased by more than 50 per cent. The depression of 1893 did not reduce the support of the schools. The depression of 1907 did not tamper with the public investment in education. And the depression of 1922 saw no educational retrenchment. It remained for the depression of 1929 to set going a process of social suicide in which a supposedly enlightened people has stood silently by while the very foundations of its education were being sapped. I have just checked over the effect of the world-wide depression on the schools of

England, France, and the Scandinavian countries. In none of these has the depression been permitted to strike the blow at education that we have permitted in the United States.

Figures have an eloquence that cannot be captured in phrases, when they are as stark and startling as the figures on the educational crisis precipitated by the American depression, but events are shifting educational statistics so rapidly that it is pointless to present them in a volume not open to almost weekly revision. It is sufficient to say that somewhere between 3,250,000 and 3,500,000 American children to-day find the door to educational advantage slammed in their faces. More than a third of these exiles from education are direct casualties of the depression. The locked doors and boarded windows of schools here and there and yonder tell this tragedy. Even the schools kept open have drastically slashed their services. Classes are crowded beyond the point of teaching efficiency and left to the mercy of teachers unpaid or underpaid. Teaching staffs are depleted as student enrollments mount. And the valid enrichments that have come to the curricula of the schools during the last quarter century are being ripped out under pressure from this interest or that ignorance to which they are but frills intolerable in a time of stringency.

Unless something comprehensively national is done, with promptitude and intelligence, to stabilize the support and stimulate the morale of the nation's educational system, we shall emerge from the depression having lost a quarter century of educational gains, and the national future will be fashioned by an inadequately disciplined people.

To date virtually no leadership, save the leadership of education itself, has gone manfully out to meet this threat to the national future. Business leadership has not. Conservative business men have, by and large, been on the side of uncritical retrenchment in educational expenditure and have applauded, here discreetly and there openly, a satirization of the teachers of the nation as parasitic tax-eaters. Political leadership has not. And the conservatism or liberalism of the leadership has not materially altered the fact of its aloofness to the issue. Despite its profound social significance, education has been largely left to shift for itself by a new-era politics that purports to put social considerations first. In face of the seeming disposition of political liberalism to insure everything to everybody, the guaranty of educational opportunity to the children of all classes and all conditions of men clamors in vain for its rightful place on the current agenda of liberal politics.

This strange slump in the national concern for education is apparently due, not to any particular social philosophy that has swept the rank and file of the people, but to an epidemic blindness to basic values that has attacked a harassed leadership in business and politics.

I assume that no extended argument is needed to prove that the crisis in economics has precipitated a crisis in education. The important thing is that the current unconcern of leadership generally with the plight of the schools be shattered by an utterly objective analysis of this plight. Without leading the layman into any wilderness of professional details, I want to suggest at least the major points of departure for such analysis.

The crisis that has caught the schools in its vise-like grip is a dual crisis. It is, on the one hand, a crisis in external support and, on the other hand, a crisis in internal policy. The sword that hangs over education is a two-edged sword. The current situation puts to society the problem of providing the schools with a financial support that will enable them adequately to carry the greatly increased load of work thrown upon them by the new freedom of children from labor and the new leisure of adults under a regime of power production which, independent of social policy, must move relentlessly toward shorter and shorter hours. The current situation puts to the schools the problem of providing society with a kind of education that will enable its men and women to master and bend to human advantage the new instrumentalities of this age of science, technology, and power production. I want now to discuss in turn these two phases of the educational crisis.

There are those who think that for educators to speak now of the dangers confronting education in the economic crisis that has chilled and arrested the national life is a kind of treason to those who are wrestling with the almost insuperable task of balancing public budgets. In the minds of such Americans, budget balancing has been lifted to the dignity of a religion, and in this improvised religion they have found mandate for the merciless inquisition of public servants who have sought to keep the national mind sensitively aware of those immediate human values and long-time social responsibilities that lie behind public budgets and for which, indeed, public budgets exist.

I cannot concur in this point of view. No one in the United States appreciates more keenly or acknowledges more readily than I the fact that institutions like individuals must tighten their belts in lean years. I have broken my lance as often as any American against waste, inefficiency, and the retention of manifestly obsolete services in government. I fought, with such weapons as were mine, for a constructively conceived economy when the economic skies were bright and the bloated statistics of a bogus prosperity tempted private individuals and public institutions alike to reckless prodigality. I think, therefore, that I have earned the right, when the economic skies are dark and the stern fact of a depleted national income confronts us, to speak of the national danger that lies coiled at the heart of educational retrenchments not dictated by a statesmanlike sense of relative values.

I am not so blind as to assume that a nation can suffer an economic dislocation so profound without its institutions having to adjust themselves to its impact. I do not suggest that, at the end of a period in which we had, in the main, so generously equipped our schools, we should not, in the midst of depression, slow down the elaboration of plant and apparatus. I do not suggest that the teacher should be exempt from his just share of the sacrifice the time may necessitate even after a broad and socially sensitive statesmanship has brought its best to the situation. Public servants who, in a phase of economic crisis, could do no more than huddle defensively around their vested interests in a frantic attempt to save their own skins and their own salaries would be unworthy of the confidence of an enlightened people.

One could not function, as I have functioned during these depression years, at so turbulent a storm-center of public expenditure as the executive headship of a large state university without vividly realizing the stark financial realities that government must face in a time of stress. But, in a phase of economic crisis, there are interests that lie beyond economics, and, unless these interests that have to do with the bodies and minds and spirits of the men and women and children of the nation are safeguarded in the midst of crisis, economic recovery itself will prove a barren achievement. It is quite as important to balance the nation's life as to balance the nation's budget. It is quite as important to prevent a social deficit for the future as to wipe out a financial deficit in the present.

The vast army of laymen who are serving on the governing boards of schools, colleges, universities, hospitals, and kindred social institutions, on city councils, in state legislatures, and in Congress are facing almost insurmountable difficulties in making ends meet. The ghost of insufficient public income persistently haunts their consideration of imperative public expenditure. Charged with the guardianship of basic public services, they must make their decisions in an atmosphere of unprecedented distraction. A thousand and one competing demands beat about their desks. They are caught in the crossfire of irrational demands for increasing public expenditures and equally irrational demands for decreasing public expenditures. They are told, in one breath, that the buying power of the period must be spread and, in the next breath, that the buying power of government must be shrunk.

If, in an atmosphere so distracting, those who must appropriate and administer public funds are to balance public budgets without unbalancing the life of community, state, and nation, they need all the help that can come from responsible and unhampered discussion of the forces and institutions upon the full and effective functioning of which the physical health, intellectual discipline, and spiritual stability of the national future must depend. To prosecute such discussion even in the midst of the direst fiscal difficulties that have confronted government in this generation is not treason but cooperation. Indeed the highest co-operation we can give to the men and women charged with the appropriation and administration of public funds is to hold so high that all may see these values that lie beyond economics, the values without which prosperity becomes a poison in the nation's vitals.

It has been part of the genius of America that we have invested liberally in education. The very liberality of this investment made it inevitable that, when depression began to enforce retrench-ment in public expenditures, there should come an unusual concentration of public attention upon the schools. No public expenditure so large can be exempt from public examination when the public income nose-dives to new low levels. Nor should it. But it is the business of statesmanship, political and economic as well as educational, to turn this depression-induced concern with the schools to constructive rather than destructive account.

In a phase of crisis, there is always a flare-up of superficial and sinister criticism of the schools and other social enterprises of government by dema-gogues who are willing to play horse with anything they think they can capitalize to their personal or political advantage. If the nation listens to such voices now, we may wreck in a year the educa-tional achievements of a quarter century. But, by and large, the common sense of our common-wealths can be trusted to take care of their dema-gogues, at least the more blatant of the breed. With this done, however, everything within our power must be done to turn to productive advantage the increasing public concern the depression has brought to bear upon our schools.

The schools are fathered and fed by the public whose instrument they are. It is the right and duty of the public to bring a sustained interest to the problem of its schools. Maximum educational progress is not realized when the public leaves the professional educator severely alone to dictate the content and determine the focus of education without let or hindrance. "Our progress in educational efficiency must come from two sources," as the late Theodore Roosevelt once rightly said, "from the great natural leader who happens to be an educator, and from the ordinary citizen who to common sense adds some power of vision, and who realizes the relation of the school to society. Therefore the ordinary citizen of vision and common sense must concern himself with the changing problem of the school, and must insist that pedantic tradition does not keep our schools from performing their full public service." Realistic educational leadership has no quarrel with the fact of an eager public interest in the schools. It wants less of demagogic attack upon the schools, but more of intelligent interest in and provocative questioning of the schools on the part of the public.

The public has certain basic rights in its schools aside from paying taxes to support them and sending its sons and daughters to them. Among the fundamental rights which the public has in its schools, rights long recognized and repeatedly stated by realistic educators, there are nine rights that have peculiar relevance to the current educational crisis.

First, the public has the right to an education that is intelligently related to the nature and needs of the contemporary life of community, state, and nation.

Second, the public has the right to an education that is flexible enough to effect progressive adjustments of its content and procedure to changing conditions in the society it serves.

Third, the public has the right to an education that produces an active rather than a passive culture, a culture that makes at once for effectiveness in private enterprise and responsibility in public service.

Fourth, the public has the right to an education that is available to all to the limit of their capacity to profit from its disciplines.

Fifth, the public has the right to an education fitted to the nature and needs of individual students. With thundering hordes of students crowding into our schools, it has been difficult enough at best to keep from factoryizing education. If we are not to factoryize American education, simplifying curriculum and classroom practice in the interest of a mass production of standardized minds, curricula must be as richly varied as the needs of students vary, and the processes of teaching must be personalized no matter how large the body of students. To trim budgets to a point where it becomes impossible to do other than present a single *table d'hôte* curriculum and herd students into large lecture halls for shotgun discharges of information, hoping against hope that some will be hit, is a short-sighted investment of public money.

Sixth, the public has the right to have its sons and daughters taught by teachers who are deeply and disinterestedly devoted to teaching as a satisfying life career, not teachers to whom teaching is but a halfway house on the road to some other and more satisfying career. The rewards of the teaching career, in the light of a lifetime, are little enough at best. The right of the public to teachers who love to teach carries with it the obligation to invest the teaching profession with a decent respect and adequate remuneration.

Seventh, the public has the right to an education it can afford. We do not live in Utopia. Month by month the bills must be met. And they cannot be met with wishes. By virtue of this uncomfortable fact, the public must retain the right to say what sort of education it can afford at any given stage of its economic development. Pseudo-leaders, in the rough-and-tumble of their demagogy, may underestimate the value of the public investment in education. It is the business of authentic leaders to expose the limited vision and selfish purposes of such misleaders of the public mind. But the right of the public to determine, in the light of honest analysis, the education it can afford remains.

Eighth, the public has the right to understand the character and cost of its schools. Schoolmen must take the mystery out of their budgets and translate their statements of educational aims into the vulgate so that what they are driving at and why it costs what it costs can be understood by taxpayers to whom the accounting terms of business offices and the technical jargon of pedagogues are all too often but so much Sanskrit.

Ninth, the public has the right to have its schools administered efficiently and economically. The mechanism of audit and report should adequately indicate the presence or absence of efficiency and economy in administration.

These, I think, are the major points around which public interest in the schools should center. But the consideration of education in this phase of depression has not been kept centered around these constructive concerns. The schools of the nation have, on the contrary, been threatened with emasculation at the hands of dishonest reductionists who have hidden in the camp of the honest advocates of essential retrenchment. The difference between the two is manifest. The honest advocates of essential retrenchment have been concerned that a sense of the centrality of education in the life of the nation be kept alive in the public mind and that, to the limit of available

[153]

resources, no effort be spared to keep the door to educational opportunity open to all classes and all conditions of the people. The dishonest reductionists, where their indifference has not been traceable to ignorance, have seemed perfectly willing to undermine public confidence in the whole system of public education if their ends could be achieved thereby.

There were solid grounds for honest alarm at the growing cost of government. But, as we swung into the depression, we were stampeded into an hysteria regarding public expenditures for such public services as education that bore all the earmarks of the hysteria that swept our sanity from its moorings during the World War. And, broadly speaking, the forces that figured most prominently in the engineering of these two aberrations of the national mind were of the same sort, namely, forces that stood to profit directly or indirectly from these hysterias.

There is an economy than can renew and an economy that can ruin nations. The economy that renews rests upon a realistic sense of relative values and an insistent putting of first things first in the investment of the available resources of government. The economy that ruins rests upon the whipping up of an indiscriminate hysteria against public expenditure for even so basic a business as caring for the bodies and cultivating the brains of the human stock for which the nation exists and through which it must function. We have seen this second sort of economy practiced throughout the United States during the last five depression years. In state after state, we have sought to balance budgets by cutting the very heart out of the only things that make government a creative social agency. We have slashed scientific bureaus. We have drastically shrunk our support of social services. We have robbed regulatory agencies of adequate resources for action. We have fired visiting nurses. We have reduced hospital staffs. We have starved libraries. We have squeezed education. We have called this economy. And we have actually thought we were intelligent in calling it that. The gods must be laughing at us. And I dislike to think of the damning indictment our grandchildren will feel when the fruits of our folly force them to remember us.

While we have been bleeding white the only things that make government socially significant, we have gone gaily on with political and economic policies that are surely setting the stage for further wars and thus fastening securely upon us three-fourths or more of the normal federal budget which goes to pay the cost of the current military establishment and to carry the obligations incurred in past wars. And state governments throughout the nation are committing the same blind sin. In our states, we lay the ax at the root of the tree of all the civilizing agencies evolved during the last half century, while we blandly tolerate a multitude of unnecessary and criminally wasteful forms of local government which, essential in the days of bottom-less mud roads and the one-horse buggy, are inde-fensible in this day of good roads, automobiles, telephones, radio, and the varied new forces that have obliterated time and distance. We could bal-ance our state budgets, and make unnecessary the surrender or starvation of a single socially significant service, if we had the insight and the courage to effect an intelligent reform of our system of local government. But to effect intelligent economies of this sort calls for a quality of thought and action we have yet to display.

In the achievement and administration of an economy that renews, a realistic educational leader-ship must cooperate to the full with the leadership of community, state, and nation. If even one drop of water can be found in any educational stock, now is the time to dehydrate. If there is anywhere in our schools a service that has outlived its use-fulness, now is the time to eliminate it. If there is any phase of the educational program that has been overdeveloped, now is the time to pull it back to reasonable dimensions. If there is, here or there, any overcoddling of the student where we might properly ask him to indulge in a little more self-education, now is the time to cut down on the spoon-feeding. And now surely is the time to declare a moratorium on those vested interests and vested ideas of the academic system that, in the most normal of times, slow down healthy processes of educational reconstruction.

But there are forces, quite outside any of these I have listed, making for an economy that ruins. I cannot but believe that the forces behind the drive for this false and fatal sort of economy are animated by three fairly clear purposes: (1) The determination of the discredited element in economic leadership to shift the blame for the depression from its own economic muddling to governmental extravagance; (2) the determination of certain interests to depress governmental expenditures to a level so low that corporate enterprise, personal incomes, and family inheritances will not face further tax drafts regardless of how drastic the drop in revenue from other sources may become; and (3) the determination of an utterly blind individualism to stop by starvation any extension of the role of the state and thus compel government to return to the simpler role of a simpler era. These, I think, have been the major motives behind the forces making for an economy that ruins, an economy that admits no consideration of relative values, but hacks blindly away at budgets in a crudely quantitative sense.

Two of the major fallacies, not to say insincerities, fostered by the type of reductionist moved by these motives deserve examination.

He will dramatically direct attention to the fact that, even before the Roosevelt regime of extraordinary expenditure set in, within the short stretch of four years, from 1928 to 1932, the tax draft on the national income rose from 11 to 33 per cent. And he will leave this statement starkly unqualified and without interpretation, quite willing that the man in the street shall uncritically infer therefrom that the cost of the public services of government had trebled in four years, and that this dramatic leap of the tax draft on national income from 11 to 33 per cent was due solely to an unintelligent and unjustified expansion of the public services of government.

Manifestly this was not true. The factor that lifted the tax draft to 33 per cent of the national income was not so much a dramatic rise in public expenditure as it was the dramatic drop in the national income from 1928 to 1933. Had the national income for 1932 remained at the 1928 level, the 1932 tax draft would have been about 18 per cent instead of 33 per cent. I am quite aware that there is no magic in mathematics than can make a 33 per cent tax draft on national income anything but a serious matter with which political, social, and economic leadership must wrestle. It plainly calls for the utmost exercise of intelligent economy if the national credit is not to take the toboggan. The facts I have just stated indicate, however, that the blame for the large proportion of the national income that was going into taxes at the end of the fourth year of depression cannot justly be placed on the shoulders of political, social, and educational leadership alone. The blunt truth is that the ineptness of an economic leadership that failed to steer the economic ship past the shoals of depression must carry a heavy share of the blame.

If this school of reductionists is permitted to go its unchallenged way in minimizing the responsibility of economic leadership for the drop in national income and magnifying the responsibility of social leadership for the rise in national expenditure, we shall see even the most disinterested public servants increasingly branded as greedy and grasping payrollers, a popular sort of propaganda which, if persisted in, will divert men of capacity and self-respect from public service for a generation to come. And it will be our children who will suffer the penalty of this diversion.

Another fallacy, fostered by the reductionist who is more interested in sabotaging government in the field of social control than in effecting constructive economies, is reflected in his subtle suggestion that every dollar that leaves the taxpayer's pocket in taxes is a dead loss to the taxpayer personally and to the business life of community, state, and nation generally. When he asserts that the fourth year of the depression saw 33 per cent of the national income go into taxes to carry the obligations and conduct the enterprises of local, state, and national government, he sedulously avoids the qualifications and interpretations that objective analysis plainly indicates. He is quite willing that the man in the street assume from his assertion that one-third of the national income was poured down a rat hole by a wastrel government.

Manifestly this was not true. We cannot know what any given tax draft upon national income means to the life of a nation until sleuth-like we have followed the tax dollar, not only as it leaves the taxpayer's pocket, but as it returns to the taxpayer's pocket. The tax dollar does, we must not forget, make a round trip. It returns by both direct and indirect routes. It goes into salaries and wages that move promptly into active circulation in payment for rent, clothing, food, gas, electric current, telephone service, street-car fare, and so on. It goes into the prompt purchase of equipment and supplies. It goes quickly back to bankers and bondholders in payment of interest and principal on bonded indebtedness of city, state, or nation. Millions that move with such rapidity cannot be set down as lost to the economic enterprise of the nation. Although publicly spent, they go to prime the pump of profitable private enterprise, quite as much as if they had been privately spent. They start industrial wheels spinning and create employment opportunity as many of the millions thrown into banks by the Reconstruction Finance Corporation have not.

It is not the unswerving insistence of this school of reductionists upon even the severest economy that endangers such basic public services as education. It is the almost blanket indictment of public servants and public services in which this school of reductionists indulges that may seriously handicap the national future. It is the subtle overtone of their plea that tends to shatter public confidence in the whole enterprise of public service. And without a vibrant and sustained public confidence, not even the most lavish budgets can bring us a productive public service.

The highest economy is productive investment, whether it be the funds of a person or the taxes of a people that are involved. It is possible to be quite as short-sighted in administering economy as in allowing extravagance. We can so easily economize blindly or let limited interests dictate the schedules of retrenchment. This is the factor that looms largest in the crisis that has struck the external support of education.

That we should resist with skeptical caution any hasty expansion of governmental activities seems to me elementary. The liberties of a free people are likely to shrink as the role of the state expands. And an expanding state must, of course, mean mounting taxes. That we must stop waste goes without saying. That we must administer the public service with the utmost economy consistent with efficiency admits of no argument. Prudence must be given a permanent seat in our public councils. But when we go to war against waste, we must be sure that it is real waste we are stopping. And we must execute our economies with broad intelligence and a sound sense of relative values.

On the Acropolis in Athens are the ruins of a lovely little temple dedicated to the Wingless

Victory. The lore of later days has it that the sculptor chiseled this symbol of victory without wings to express the hope of the Athenians that victory would never again fly from their city. The victory it celebrated is now forgotten of men, save as the antiquarians may salvage its story. And the temple itself is now a scarred ruin. But its mute existence leads us to ask what victories of ancient Greece have stayed and what have been snatched away? And it needs no new research to frame the answer. The victories of Athens and of its empire that were victories of sheer force, physical or political, notable as they were at the time, have gone from the minds of all save the historians. But the victories won by the Greeks who were pathfinders of the mind and spirit, the philosophers and poets and dramatists and historians who expressed the Greek passion for truth and beauty and goodness, these victories have been wingless. They have never left Greece. The Greeks who dealt in deathless values themselves became deathless, and in myriad ways their legacy still lives to water the parched roots of the world's culture and the world conscience.

History has unforgettably dramatized the problem of relative values in the story of Athens. The transient values of force, the power of organized interests, concerned with material conquest, and the lust for supremacy, seductive to many at the time, have lost in the court of history. It has always been so. It is so now. It will be so for all time. But man is a stubborn and singularly obtuse animal. He declines to listen to the record. He persists in pursuing victories that will surely fly from him once he wins them. And he spends his life in quest of achievements that he should know will turn to ashes in his mouth.

Here is a parable for statesmen, whether the day's work sets for them the task of balancing a budget or reconstructing a social order. In the midst of fiscal difficulties and economic dilemmas, no matter how dire, we must keep our attention tethered to those deathless values that give enduring greatness to a civilization. And wingless victories can be won, even in the midst of the most drastic retrenchment that necessity may enforce, if we administer our economies with bold intelligence instead of blind hysteria.

In the decisions it makes respecting its support of education, the nation is dealing with one of the deathless values of civilization, a value more vital to the complex civilization of this modern phase than to any civilization of simpler centuries. If the nation is short-sighted in the decisions it makes, it cannot confine the wages of its sin to the generation that blunders. We can defer the building of a road, a bridge, or a building and catch up on its construction later. We cannot put educational opportunity for the millions in cold storage for the duration of a depression and restore it later to an unschooled generation grown old. These must go through life a lost generation poisoning the processes of popular thought and political action with their undisciplined judgments.

So much for the crisis in the external support of education. I turn now to the crisis in the internal policy of the schools. And here the crisis is quite as real.

During the last quarter century, the civilization going on outside the walls of our schools has changed profoundly under the impact of the forces of science, technology, and power production, and has put a bewildering array of new problems to the individual American as well as to business, industry, finance, the church, the state, and the family. The rapidity and revolutionary nature of this social change have taxed, almost beyond the point of effective response, the capacity of the schools for flexible adjustment of the content and procedures of education to the new circumstances of this new civilization for life in which they must contrive to train.

Schools do not operate in a vacuum. They function at the center of a swirl of forces that are forever churning and changing the nature and mood of the age. They could not, if they would, stay aloof from the processes of conflict and change that surge through the social order they seek to serve.

In the quarter century before the onset of the depression in 1929, the schools of the United States had the difficult job of playing guardian to the complementary forces of stability and progress in a phase of profound flux. At least seven silent but sweeping revolutions were remaking, for good or for ill, the life around our schools.

A political revolution was under way. Self-centered national governments were failing to solve the international problems of the twentieth century. War was assuming an aspect of universal destructiveness. A call to some sort of world organization sounded insistently above the cries of our separate patriotisms. We have since slumped back into a phase of tribalism, but, for a time, the minds of men, at least, clutched at concepts that went beyond tribalism. And everywhere the mass man crowded to the center of the stage with dictatorships and democracies alike bidding for his favor. Democracy was no longer the regnant religion it once was. New and alien philosophies of strong government found fertile soil in the bewilderment of the post-war years.

An industrial revolution was under way. The competition between machine power and man power raced on with increasing intensity. A famine of employment opportunity that could not be charged to an Act of God loomed as a permanent possibility of the power age. The power to produce was fast exceeding the power to purchase. New technical processes were rendering old economic policies obsolete. Extensive social readjustments were becoming imperative. And foreign policy, as well as domestic economy, was involved. Super-power and mass production were making active

[165]

international markets, stabilized by some sort of world coordination, more and more necessary.

A financial revolution was under way. The determining economic power of the world was rapidly getting out from under the dominance of European politics and was coming under the thumb of American business. Markets were becoming financially less dependent upon wealth and more dependent upon wages for stable continuity. There was a progressive broadening of the base of stock ownership, with some momentary influence upon the psychology of capital and labor, if but little influence upon actual industrial control. The old formulas alike of wealth and of ownership were in process of change. As the modern economy of science, technology, and power production matured, wealth became less and less a static something to be captured and cached, and was increasingly regarded as a dynamic something that must be continuously created and recreated. At least so regarded by all who were alive to the forces of economic modernism. As the process of corporate development marched ahead, the most astute analysts of the modern corporation saw it making for ownership without control and control without ownership. Wealth went dynamic and ownership went impersonal.

A scientific revolution was under way. Men pushed their mastery of nature further and further. As they established a firmer and firmer scientific control over their physical environment, they leaned less heavily on forms of religious authority that arose out of some dim past when men faced nature with fear rather than understanding. Science was changing men's minds in this and a thousand other ways, even if the science of the laboratory seemed but slowly to influence the statecraft of the legislature. And the lives of men were being subtly changed by the seemingly inexhaustible flow of new machines, new instruments, new appliances, as the science-born automobile, for example, altered the social habits of the world.

A religious revolution was under way. Multitudes of modern men were finding difficulty in adjusting themselves effectively to the modernisms of science and social organization in terms of historic creeds and dogmas. The diverse racial faiths were coming more and more into contact, and each was feeling the impact of the others. There was increasing impatience with a religion insulated from the issues that intimately color and control men's lives. With race hatreds, wars, and revolutions on their horizon, men were groping for a religious experience that would help them meet the problems thrown up out of the competition of races, nations, and classes.

A psychological revolution was under way. Men were slipping the leash of intellectual traditions, group ideals, personal codes, and social disciplines that had long gone unquestioned. On the part of millions there was a rather complete mental and emotional break with the past. The equilibrium of the outer and inner forces of men's lives was disturbed. And, despite the varied poses of unconcern that were for a time fashionable, men were concerned to find a new and better balance.

A social revolution was under way. The individual was being superseded by the group as the important unit in policy and action. The small local community, with the autonomy and richness of life that once marked it, was passing. There was a steady migration of competence from countryside to city. America was going urban with astounding rapidity. The center of economic gravity was shifting from agriculture to industry. The old fluidity of classes showed signs of freezing, although the poor could still climb to the seats of power by the grace of superlative capacity. The new economics was putting to the old politics problem for which there were no answers in the textbooks. The masses were beginning to sense what they might do to better their economic lot through the use of their political power, while radio, motion pictures, the talking film, and the airplane were beginning profoundly to affect the social outlook.

These few brush strokes, in lieu of a completer picture, give some sense of the flux and ferment in the society our schools had to serve in the quarter century before 1929. In so mercurial a situation, it was no easy matter to determine wisely just what and how the schools should teach. But one thing was clear, namely, that processes of change so profound and so pervasive made necessary a conscious reconsideration of the content and procedures of education in terms of what these seven revolutions were doing to American life and to the lives of Americans. For the better part of that quarter century, however, there were special circumstances that made popular pressure for such reconsideration less insistent than it might have been. First the single-track concentration of the war years and then the lotus-eating mood of the era of speculation diverted the public mind from any absorbing concern with the social adjustment of our basic institutions.

To-day the situation is the exact reverse. The depression has intensified all the more basic trends of the seven revolutions that were under way before the economic collapse. It has generated in us an extraordinary willingness to subject our traditional policies and institutions to critical reconsideration. And it has exposed, with compelling effect, how far behind social change many of our social institutions have lagged.

It is always a critical moment in the history of social institutions when the civilization they were designed to serve shifts the bases of its thought and action. It is in such moments that historic institutions may either find renewal or be relegated to limbo. If the adjustment of social institutions to the social change surrounding them is inadequate or unduly laggard, they may find themselves

[169]

suddenly bereft of their traditional support, summarily changed by external authority, or sweepingly disestablished and supplanted by alternative agencies through which society thinks it can better achieve its aims. If, on the other hand, social institutions adjust themselves intelligently to the social change surrounding them, they may experience a fresh invigoration and enter a phase of productive development.

It is some such situation that to-day confronts the schools, colleges, and universities of the United States. And their directive leadership may profitably review the historic record of institutions that have failed fully to reckon with the phenomenon of social change outside their walls.

The enterprise of education has bulked about as large in twentieth century America as the enterprise of religion bulked in the Europe of the Middle Ages. And the educational establishments of modern America now face a situation that bears at least a limited likeness to the situation that confronted the religious establishments of medieval Europe preceding their phase of decline. Schoolmen may with profit reexamine the fate of the religious foundations of the Middle Ages and reflect upon the maladjustment between their internal policies and the external circumstances of the time which resulted in their downfall. They failed to meet constructively the changes that went on without their walls.

Schoolmen may with equal profit reexamine the record of the impact of the French Revolution upon the French universities. Here, again, is evidence of what happens to social institutions when they fail to take fully into account changes in the climate of opinion surrounding them. The surface symptoms of the American readjustment now in process are far from identical with the violent manifestations of the French Revolution, but we are confronted with reconstructions of political, social, and economic policy quite as basic even if bloodless. The corporate form to which France had entrusted the interests of the higher learning had lost the capacity for flexible adjustment to changes in the social situation it was designed to serve. The result was that, from the outset of the Revolution, the universities were heckled and harassed by the political authorities. Here and there their property was seized. Their independent status and corporate privileges were revoked. Professional tests were abolished. And, finally, on September 15, 1793, the convention sweepingly suppressed "the colleges and the faculties of theology, medicine, arts, and law over all the surface of the Republic." This suppression was suspended within twenty-four hours, but seventeen months later the colleges were definitely abolished by decree. The French universities, like the monasteries of an earlier time, failed to meet constructively the changes that went on without their walls. And the result was that the French

Revolution scrapped the French universities and set itself to the task of educational reconstruction from the outside.

The likelihood of anything so sweeping may be remote, but it is not, in my judgment, impossible that the story of the monasteries and the French universities will be repeated in the course of the American readjustment into which events are forcing the government and enterprise of the United States. There is, at any rate, enough in the analogy to bring everyone concerned with the preservation and promotion of a valid education promptly to attention.

I am keenly aware of the superficiality of much of the criticism that has lately been lodged at the doors of the educators, but I refuse to blind myself to the fact that there is a spreading disillusionment with the content and focus of an education that has not produced a leadership better equipped to keep the social and economic orders from running amuck. As the breakdown in social management, from which we along with the rest of the Western peoples are suffering, becomes more and more manifest, the conviction grows that the general impact of our education upon popular judgment and the thinking of leadership has been as unsatisfactory as its technical training for specialized enterprise has been satisfactory.

In my *Thunder and Dawn*, in a chapter on Educating for Social Mastery, I went at length into the grounds for this growing disillusionment, and found myself forced to agree with the critics of my craft in their contention that, while Western education has been superbly successful in training Western man for the technical execution of his separate enterprises, it has signally failed to fit him for realistic statesmanship in the ground plan and governance of his social and economic orders, and that, through the last quarter century, the fruits of this failure have been evident in a generation of leaders whose fingers have all been thumbs in the molding of those general policies of political, social, and economic organization which, in the end, make or break the separate enterprises of men.

"And, although it pains me as a schoolman to admit it," I wrote, "I cannot but believe that Western education must share the blame for this breakdown of political, social, and economic organization. We are reaping the Dead Sea fruits of an era of over-specialization in Western education. . . . And we have produced what we have thus been organized educationally to produce, namely, a generation of specialists. The vast crowd of customers who enter and leave the schools of the West without becoming good specialists nevertheless bear the mark of the system in their minds. They are partialists who are powerless to play a constructive role in the analysis and adjustment of a social order whose current instability is to be found at the point of the relationships of its parts. With a mind molded by specialized instruction, Western man everywhere displays an increasing reluctance to wrestle with difficult problems as a whole. He dismembers his difficulties and sends their separate parts to the appropriate specialists. And then, when his social order faces a general crisis, as now, he finds the specialists unwilling, even in consultation, to assume responsibility for general conclusions."

I wrote this in 1931 before either the National Socialism of Germany or the New Deal of the United States had been added to the Communism of Russia and the Fascism of Italy in seeming contradiction of the contention that Western man is reluctant and ill-equipped to deal with difficult problems as a whole, because his education has been essentially the education of a specialist, and that the specialists decline responsibility in the field of general policy. But the more I burrow into the current process of political experimentalism the more I am convinced that the contention holds in the sense that the overspecialized education of these later years has not adequately equipped us for the prompt mastery of the problem of social management that the economy of science, technology, and power production has now put to us.

With us, indeed, the national problem has been tackled as a whole, and the specialists have come out of their separate cells of expertness and gone at the building of broad policies with an unprecedented abandon. But it is obvious, I think, that desperation rather than a sense of confident grasp has driven us to the ambitious ventures in national planning upon which we have lately entered. And, as we put this planning under the microscope, it becomes clear that its net result to date is not so much a national plan as a medley of divergent and mutually contradictory plans, as, for example, the plan to increase wages has been nullified by the plan to increase prices.

In theory, the national leadership is planning. In practice, it is playing by ear. I do not quarrel with this. Playing by ear may not be so bad a thing, in a phase of unprecedented uncertainty, if the player has a good ear for music. It can, however, land us in confusion worse confounded. And, if a leadership that is playing by ear hypnotizes itself into the belief that it is planning, it can quickly degenerate into a rigid dogmatism that is sure it has in its bag the one remedy that will cure all of our ills in thirty days or money refunded. That is infinitely more dangerous than the frankest of catch-as-catch-can improvising.

And, finally, the dependability of the judgment of specialists in the field of general policy is still to be proved. We may well find that it is simply not safe to turn the financial experts loose on monetary policy, the economic experts loose on industrial policy, and the social experts loose on budgetary policy without the correlating genius of a broadly educated statesmanship to correct their conclusions in terms of their interaction in practical operation. We cannot put the single-track policies of specialists from varied fields together like flag-stones and expect effective national policy to be the result. Effective national policy is not a mosaic of separate judgments. It is a living force that functions as a unity.

It is just this genius for correlation, this capacity to see the interrelation of separate and specialized judgments, and this trained ability to ferret out the social implications of knowledge that the education of the last quarter century or more has been least effective in fostering. The sense that this is so lies at the root of the educational disillusionment that has fallen upon so many of the abler minds of the time.

Added to this skepticism of traditional education at the more select levels of judgment, there is to-day a special factor that gravely threatens the popular enthusiasm for education which has here-tofore been a distinguishing mark of the American temper. I refer to the long and lean army of school, college, and university graduates who have tasted the bitter bread of insecurity and had their spirits broken on the rack of unemployment. I have seen the inside of the minds of hundreds of these men during the last five years. And, as one concerned with the maintenance of a fruitful social attitude toward the enterprise of education, I do not like what I have seen there.

In the long hours of enforced idleness, these men have tightened their belts, and let their minds run reminiscently back over the long years of school, college, and university education that have left them workless in a world of closed doors. They are to-day, by and large, centers of dissatisfaction with the content and focus of American education. They are not irrational enough to assume that formal schooling can ever become an infallible insurance against unemployment for every man with a diploma or degree. They do not assume that the universities can magically stabilize the turbulence of this transition into a new world of science, technology, and power production. But, in a half-wistful half-resentful mood, they do feel that the whole social situation might be different to-day if, during the last few decades, the schools, colleges, and universities, in their curricular arrangements and teaching procedures, had attacked more directly the problem of giving their graduates a living and informed sense of the forces and tendencies that have combined to give this historic juncture in American affairs its peculiar and perilous character.

They dimly sense what seems to me the obvious fact, namely, that a generation of Americans that had been consciously and comprehensively grounded by the schools in an understanding of the forces that were currently making, unmaking, and remaking the political, social, and economic orders would, in general, have reacted with a more flexible intelligence to the political and economic issues of the time and would have thrown up out of its ranks a more realistic leadership that would

[177]

have been less content to let affairs drift relentlessly toward the debacle of 1929. And this, they feel, would well have been worth the sacrifice, if necessary, of much that has been traditional in the objectives and content of American education.

The reaction of these unemployed and the more conscious analysis of the educational realist alike underscore the fact that the situation now confronting American educators cannot be met by any mere reshuffling of the cards in curricula. The problem involved is nothing less than a fresh determination of what the directive aim of American education shall be in the light of the new nature and the new needs of the new civilization brought into being on this continent by the forces of science, technology, and power production, a civilization in which social change has so far outstripped institutional change as to throw the survival of our social order in the shadow of serious doubt.

(Many of the patterns of our educational system, like many of the patterns of our political and economic orders, were designed in terms of the simpler and more highly personalized life of the pioneer era. And, to a degree that seems to some indefensible, they reflect also an era in which education was predominantly a source of passive culture for a leisure class and of preparation for the learned professions. (The schools must still keep going that relay race of the human spirit in which, from generation to generation, the seasoned wisdom and matured beauty of the centuries are handed on.

For the learned professions the schools must now provide a richer and more rigid training than ever before. But the life that made these the dominant, if not exclusive, demands upon education is not the life of contemporary America. And to the degree that we persist in educating for social situations that no longer exist, we depress the effectiveness of education and intensify every latent skepticism of its processes.

This is the heart of the crisis in internal policy that has struck American education. The crisis in external support is, in some measure, related to this crisis in internal policy. It is related at least in the sense that an education steered by a thoroughly modernized directive aim, brought more immediately to focus on the political, social, and economic problems of contemporary America, and animated by the avowed social purpose of training a generation of citizens to play a productive role in the creation, comprehension, and control of a workable order of life in an age of plenty will renew and reenforce in the American mind its early, if then somewhat uncritical, belief that, in the words of the ancient Talmud, "by the breath of the schoolchildren shall the state be saved." And a people so convinced will not long tolerate a crisis in the external support of its educational enterprise.

VII

RELIGION EXILED

AMONG Western nations on the hunt for
sources of national renewal, it remained for
Germany most vividly to dramatize the
fact that religion is among the factors of vitaliza-
tion with which a truly inclusive leadership must
deal.

I do not mean to suggest that I have any
sympathy with Herr Hitler's attempt politically to
regiment the churches of Germany. I have not. A
people stands to gain nothing and to lose much by
the conversion of its clergy into uncritical press
agents of the political aims of a transient regime. I
have no first-hand knowledge either of Nazi purposes
or of Nazi procedures in the attempt virtually to
create a national church. The motive of the move
may have been narrowly secular and the manner of
its execution reprehensible. Quite aside from either
the motive or the manner of his action, however,
there is the force of fruitful suggestion in the fact
that Herr Hitler, as Chancellor of the Reich,
turned to religion as one of the major factors in the
rebirth of the German spirit and the renewal of the
German state. His action has at least raised afresh
the question of the role of religion in the life of the

state. And we may thank Herr Hitler for having raised the question, even if the answer he suggests is the essence of folly.

There is an important distinction between regimenting the churches for the political advantage of a government and resorting to the religious impulse as an energizing force and factor of cohesion in the social renewal of a national life. The political regimentation of the churches is, on every ground, both indefensible and self-defeating. The church, like the school, must, if it is to have productive meaning in the life of the time, maintain freedom of action without aloofness of interest in the conflicts that center in the state. I have argued elsewhere that, while it is part of the business of school and church to supply the state with the raw materials of fact and ideal for a creative politics, it is not the business of either school or church to become entangled in the political task of compromise, which is the business of the state. When they do become so entangled, the professors and the parsons often prove no more adept than the politicians at statecraft, and, becoming absorbed in the chess play of politics, they tend to let the intellectual and moral reservoirs of politics run dry. Despite this distinctiveness of function, school and church and state have a common interest in the common enterprise of creating a humanly meaningful national life, but the mistake must not be made of attempting to coerce this unity of aim into uniformity of approach.

Even the wisest relating of church and state, however, does not solve the problem of the role of religion in the life of a people. How to keep church and state separate without insensibly underestimating the contribution a vital religion may make to the maintenance of meaning and morale in the national life is a dilemma no modern people has yet resolved.

The *de facto* union of church and state that often exists alongside a *de jure* separation of church and state is surely not the answer to the problem. To a degree we dislike to admit, in times of calm, the church tends to go subordinate to the forces dominant in the economic order. The corporate courage of movements that intermittently question the ethics of established economic policies and the individual bravery of scattered prophets who live in scorn of the small safeties of conformity are variant from the rule. And, to a degree we dislike to admit, in times of crisis, the church tends to go subordinate to the forces dominant in the political order. When war is in the air, for example, and the state barks, the church ordinarily barks and begins lustily to hunt with the pack. When the state drafts its citizens, the church drafts its god, clothes him in khaki, and sends him to the front. If the crudity of this sentence smacks of irreverence, its irreverence of form but reflects the irreverence of fact it records. This too facile surrender of the church to the economic order, in times of calm, and to the political order, in times of crisis, is no answer to the problem of religion in the national life.

The psalm-singing captains of industry, once more numerous than now, whose piety and practicality never quite mesh, can hardly be held the symbol of vital religion operative in the national life. Some years ago a well-known American, at once a devoted churchman and a distinguished captain of industry, spent two hours ardently defending the twelve-hour day in one of our basic industries, and closed his defence of this indefensible policy by warmly recommending Bible reading and a revival of old-time religion as a solvent of our social difficulties. This does not so much as skirt the problem of the role of religion in the life of a people. It is this concept of religion as an aloof pietism, utterly divorced from the sweat and struggle of the day's work, that has led the extremer radicalisms of the time to list religion among the opiates.

Nor has the parson turned lobbyist given us the answer to the problem of how best to release the productive power of religion in the renewal and stabilization of a national life, despite the fact that he has been on the job for some time. The political parson is not a new figure in history. He looms along the secular skyline throughout the centuries.

He appears in the long line of Hebrew prophets who, with the social imagination of a Wells and the stinging irony of a Shaw, dealt with the political and economic practices of their time quite

[183]

in the manner of our best modern publicists. As
spokesman of the young religion of Christianity, in
the first and second centuries, he fostered in its
adherents a kind of attitude and activity that
troubled the rulers of the state and stirred them to
retaliation through wholesale persecution. The
eighth century finds him drawing the fire of the
more conventional religious leadership because he
persisted in poking his nose into the dark corners
of the social order and insisting that religion should
light and disinfect them. The Middle Ages find him
struggling to establish a churchly sovereignty over
the whole of human affairs throughout the world.
The Reformation reveals him involved quite as
deeply in the political ambitions of princes and the
economic hungers of peasants as in the philosophical
revision of theological patterns and the practical
reform of church practices. The Puritan movement
of the post-Reformation period found him active.
And American politics has had to reckon with him.

To say that the parson turned lobbyist does not
adequately symbolize the role of religion in the
life of a nation is not to say that religion is a thing
apart from the day's affairs or that the church
should not concern itself with the moral values at
stake in the way men live and make their living,
rear their families, conduct their schools, run their
businesses, practice their professions, and rule
their governments. It is only to say that the church,
in its more secular reform ventures, has often
hindered rather than hastened the supremacy of

[184]

spiritual values in human affairs. When the church has followed an irresponsible fanaticism rather than an intelligent statesmanship, when it has created a swarm of new evils by the way it has sought to cure a single old evil, when it has acted on the Machiavellian assumption that the end justifies the means and achieved its reforms by methods regarded as reprehensible when employed by the ward politicians, it can hardly be said that the role of religion in the life of the state has been well played.

It may seem to some beside the point to inject the problem of religion into a consideration of the political, social, and economic stimulation and stabilization of American life. Let me say why I think it is not. In general, it is important that we preserve, as a sweetening and savoring factor in our national life, certain priceless values, immemorially associated with religion undefiled, which are gravely endangered in this phase of disillusionment. But there is a special circumstance at the current juncture in American affairs that makes extraordinarily important the role of religion in the renewal of American life and enterprise. It is this special circumstance, which I want now to consider, that has led me to include in this study of the American outlook this brief statement of a point of view respecting religion.

The traditional order of American life and enterprise has come definitely to a crossroads where we must choose between a voluntary cooperation of all classes and all interests for common ends and submission to a regime of compulsion which, in its efforts to break the stalemate of the last five years, will impose upon us an increasingly detailed schedule of political and economic demands. No authentic American wants to see compulsion come. The essence of the American spirit is its love of freedom. If the American is to maintain his traditional freedom of life and enterprise, he must now give attention to the conditions upon which freedom is feasible in the current phase of our economic evolution, and he must consider with an utterly open mind such revisions in the method of freedom as the nature of the age may have made imperative.

There are only two regimes under which free men can live happily: a regime of extreme laissez faire or a regime of control through a wide and willing cooperation. Extreme laissez faire works well in a simple society, and free men enjoy stretching their powers unhindered. Extreme laissez faire does not work well in a complex society, and sooner or later free men find their freedom worthless in the midst of a crashing collapse of their enterprise. Having practiced the liberty of extreme laissez faire for so long, free men, when caught in a major collapse of their economic order, rush distractedly about, with next to no disciplined capacity for that prompt cooperation for common ends which becomes the price of recovery and stabilization. And, in their distraction, they all too often fall wistfully into the arms of dictatorship.

This is the story of Russia. This is the story of Italy. This is the story of Germany. It has threatened to be the story of many an erstwhile stable people. Will it be the story of the United States?

One thing, more than any other single factor, can insure us against surrender to an increasing measure of compulsion. And that is the awakening throughout the country of a determination, essentially religious in the passion of its purpose, to weld individuals, groups, and classes everywhere into a vast and conscious cooperative ordering of the national life in terms of the common welfare of its whole people.

Despite the seeming abstractness of this assertion, there is nothing nebulous here. It may, indeed, be more practical than any practical politics we have yet mustered. We have, I suspect, come to a juncture in our affairs at which, if we are promptly to adopt and widely to apply those socially sound policies of enterprise which alone can bring economic stability in a power age, we shall have to tap deeper levels of social determination than political or economic leadership normally taps. This, it seems to me, is the major challenge the American situation now puts to spiritual leadership.

This is not asking the church to venture outside its legitimate jurisdiction or bending religion to base kitchen usage. The church stands in the minds of men as the interpreter, guardian, and promoter of spiritual values. Spiritual values do not, however, appear from nowhere and hang suspended in thin air. They appear and are expressed, as I have said, in the way men live and make their living, rear their families, conduct their schools, run their businesses, practice their professions, and rule their governments. Save in terms of a mystic sainthood that hides itself from abrasive contact with the rough edges of life as it is lived by the generality of men, spiritual values can be promoted only in and through these basic social enterprises of banks, business houses, farms, factories, schools, homes, and the state which binds these institutions into the organic unity of a national life. If the church is to be more than a merchandise mart for pale abstractions, it must maintain an intimate and continuous moral analysis of these political, social, and economic processes of contemporary society. How otherwise can it offer to modern men that expertness of judgment on the moral meanings of modern life and enterprise which they rightly ask? To ask spiritual leadership to play a productive role in the secular struggle for national recovery and stabilization is not, therefore, asking it to venture outside its legitimate jurisdiction.

In particular, it is not asking the church to exceed its inherent function when its leadership is challenged, as here, to captain a crusade for the universal cooperation of individuals, groups, and classes in a determined national search for the policies and practices that will make our vast mechanisms of science, technology, and power production servant instead of sovereign to the

human spirit. The church may justly be indicted
for impertinence when it seeks to dictate the
details of business management or determine the
personnel of government, but the church is never
nearer to its function than when it is setting large
and morally significant goals before the people of
the nation it serves. The active guardianship and
promotion of moral values in the secular ventures
of politics and economic enterprise are among the
major obligations of spiritual leadership. When,
about a century ago, the incomparable Mazzini
was preaching to the Italy of his time the gospel
of the duties of man as the imperative complement
of the gospel of the rights of man, he was rendering
a sort of ministry to the secular life of man which
society may rightly ask from the church. Had the
Italy of Mazzini's time been building a Bible, his
flaming pronouncements would surely have con-
stituted one of the Books of the Prophets.

In the current American situation, the combined
forces of Catholicism, of Protestantism, and of the
whole run of fellowships that variations of race and
reason have fostered, augmented by all the anony-
mous religious concern that may reside in our
people, should, if the contentions I have advanced
are sound, now come to focus on the stimulation of
a vast and vigorous folk-movement for the reconsideration and redirection of our political,
social, and economic energies through a nation-wide
cooperation in which personal and class interests
are adjourned and the increase, enrichment, and

stabilization of life for the millions made the dominant concern of the directive leadership of business, industry, finance, and government. In so doing, the church would be dealing, not with the secular details, but with the spiritual dynamic, of national recovery and stabilization.

It may be said that the clergy and the more active lay leadership of the church are not intimately enough conversant with the technical complexity of the problems of business, industry, finance, and government to make sure that the stirring of such folk-movement would not cause more troubles than it cured. This doubt is understandable, but it lacks validity. It rests upon a misconception of the field in which spiritual leadership is here asked to function.

In the light of the record, since the forces of science, technology, and power production began fully to register their effects upon the enterprise of the Western world, the same doubt might meet the suggestion that economic leadership now undertake consciously to humanize and stabilize our power economy. We are here dealing with ends rather than means, and, while the economic leadership that has lately had its hands on the levers of power has been superbly expert in the manipulation of means, it has been incredibly short-sighted in the establishment of ends. In the matter of determining the broad social objectives of industrialism, the practical man has failed even to pursue policies of intelligent self-interest. His obsolescent philosophy of wages, hours, prices, and profits has sabotaged the productive machine his genius created, and stalled it at a time when the singing rhythm of its wheels should be answering with uncurbed production the cry of unsatisfied human need which, despite the current delusion of surplus, sounds insistently through the walls of its factories.

If the hand of economic leadership could but be forced by a folk-movement to the general adoption of wage, hour, price, and profit policies that would effect a generous spread of income and establish a socially sound margin of mass leisure, economic leadership would find, not that it had been victimized by a proletarian robbery, but that it had been pushed by popular pressure into the only policies that can insure the survival and permanent profitability of capitalistic industrialism in a power age, the mass production of which is self-defeating unless industrialism itself assures mass consumption through socially sound economic policies.

And, if these ends could but be achieved under the compulsion of the sort of folk-movement I have suggested, spiritual leadership would find, not that the concern of mankind had become exclusively absorbed in a secular revel in comforts and luxuries, but that the national life had become a soil from which the subtler values of the spirit would flower.

In other words, if the contention I have advanced is true, namely, that the future of the social order may be profoundly enriched by a vital religion, it is equally true that the future of religion may be richly advanced by a valid social order. The future of American religion and the future of the American social order are more intimately interlocked than many, in the facile modernism of their thinking, have been inclined to believe. Quite apart, then, from any direct concern with the secular issues of national recovery, spiritual leadership cannot effectively safeguard and stimulate the spiritual interests of which it is, in a special sense, protector and promoter without plunging manfully into the business of hammering the organization of our political, social, and economic forces into social soundness. The events of the time make clear that this is true. To illustrate the impact that a nation's social order may have upon a nation's religion, let me go to an issue that may seem far afield from our current absorption in the secular problems of national recovery and stabilization, the issue of the spread of atheism.

The spiritual leadership of the church is deeply concerned over the widespread secession from belief in God that has been increasingly evident as the age of scientific control over natural forces has come to maturity. Despite the innumerable modernisms of belief to which my mind gives allegiance, I share this concern. I know the barbarisms and indignities that fanatics have perpetrated in the name of God. I know the innumerable caricatures that short-sighted men have drawn of his countenance, reading their own lusts and limitations into his purposes. I know how, creating him out of the clay of their own being, whole peoples have projected the tyranny or tenderness of their social orders into their concept of God. I know how often sinister interests have sought to use God as a smoke screen for their selfish adventures. But I know also the myriad army of saints and seers whose lives, illuminated by an exalted concept of God, have been given to fertilize the soil from which the freedom, as well as the faith, of mankind has flowered. And I am convinced, alike by the historic record and by contact with the affairs of my time, that a civilization that exiles an exalted concept of God from its heart dries up one of the major well-springs of its power.

I agree with the stimulant vision of Edna St. Vincent Millay when, in her *Renascence and Other Poems*, she affirms the indispensable value to life of a vibrant faith that the universe is instinct with meaning.

> Not Truth, but Faith, it is
> That keeps the world alive. If all at once
> Faith were to slacken—that unconscious Faith
> Which must, I know, yet be the corner stone
> Of all believing—birds now flying fearless
> Across would drop in terror to the earth;
> Fishes would drown; and the all-governing reins
> Would tangle in the frantic hands of God
> And the worlds gallop headlong to destruction.

Remote as their relation may seem to the practicalities of social and economic renewal, here are questions quite as vital to the national future as industrial codes and trade agreements: How shall spiritual leadership make God again believable to men who have lost all faith in any lordship of life? How shall we save men of this generation from a corrosive cynicism? How shall we help disillusioned men to recapture a courageous confidence that life is not a blind dance of atoms, but a meaningful adventure worthy of deathless objectives? These are questions that should concern the statesman quite as much as the theologian. They have vital secular import because men bereft of confidence and blinded by cynicism do not build creative civilizations.

But, granted the reality of the problem, how are we to achieve the conquest of cynicism and the restoration of confidence? I shall not presume to make final answer to questions which, like these, have harassed mankind since the infancy of the race. In the presence of these questions, however, I feel sure of one thing, namely, that few, if any, modern men are either drawn to belief or driven into disbelief in God and a universe instinct with meaning by the traditional dialectics of the theists and atheists. Men's belief in God and a meaningful universe is buttressed or broken less by the arguments they hear than by the way in which the social order, in which they have to live, buttresses or breaks their lives.

This contention is poignantly enforced by two episodes that have etched themselves indelibly upon my mind. The first is the story of Job in the

Old Testament. The other is the story of Peer Tröen in Johan Bojer's *The Great Hunger*.

Job was a man of devout faith. He was a man of means, but prosperity had not softened him or lured him from loyalty to those values that lie beyond economics. No slightest shadow of infidelity to his belief that the universe was meaningful and under the sovereignty of a God of Justice darkened his outlook. But disaster came to test the temper of the man. The Arabs stole his asses and slew his servants attending them. Lightning struck and burned to a cinder his sheep, his goats, and his shepherds. The Chaldeans robbed him of his camels and killed his camel drivers. A whirlwind struck dead his seven sons and three daughters as they wined and dined. And his own body was blighted with ulcers and racked with pain. For a time he clung stubbornly to his confidence in the sovereign justice of his universe, but finally the impact of his external misfortunes upon his internal attitudes crushed his confidence. And, although he later found his way back to his old confidence, Job suffered a transient slump into cynicism as a result of his secular troubles.

His own description of the secular source of his religious apostasy, as it may be pieced together from scattered sentences out of James Moffatt's vividly modern translation of this immortal drama, has pertinence to the contention I have advanced that the confidence or cynicism with which men face the ultimate issues of destiny and the govern-

[195]

ance of the universe may be but a reflection of
what society has done to their lives.

After listening to Job's tirade against his fate
and seeing the cynicism that was falling over his
traditionally confident spirit, Eliphaz the Temanite,
one of three friends who had come to comfort him,
sought to bring Job's spirit back to normal.

"Passion like that is futile, fatal," said Eliphaz.
"Let your religion reassure you."

"Passion?" cried Job. "Compare my passion of
despair with the full weight of my calamity! It is
heavier than the sands of the sea. That makes my
words so wild. . . . Does a wild ass bray when he
has grass? . . . I am forced to live empty months,
and nights of misery are allotted me. . . . Illusions
are indeed my lot; I face the bitter mockery of
life. . . . What strength have I to hold out?
What is before me, that I should be patient? Is my
strength equal to the strength of stones, is my flesh
made of bronze? No, there is no help, none; and all
aid has abandoned me. . . . I am sick, sick of
life. . . . I will restrain myself no longer; I will
speak out, so bitter is my soul."

These words have a strangely contemporary
sound, as if they had been spoken from some
street-corner rostrum last night and reported in this
morning's press. They might, indeed, have been
spoken by millions throughout the Western world
in these years when economic insecurity and social
instability have been playing havoc with their
lives. The weight of their calamity has been heavy.

They have lived empty months and gone sleepless through nights made miserable by fear. Illusions have been their lot. Life has looked at them with a bitter mockery. And their strength has not always equaled the strength of stones. Bitterness has eaten acidlike into the souls of many. And, sick of life as affairs have forced them to live it, their words, like Job's, have sometimes gone wild. The months that have been empty of economic security have emptied their lives of the old confidence, and cynicism has rushed in to fill the void.

Surely this impact of current circumstances upon the human spirit is a matter of major concern to the religious leadership of the time. And anything religious leadership can do to modulate and humanize this impact is not leading it outside its legitimate field. Job displayed an insight, needed now alike by statesmen and by churchmen, into the intimate relation that exists between the secular life and the spiritual attitude of a people, when he said, "Friends should be kind to a despairing man, or he will give up faith in the Almighty."

The story of Peer Tröen, in Johan Bojer's *The Great Hunger*, enforces by positive action the same fact that the story of Job illustrates by negative reaction. At the end of Peer Tröen's odyssey of the spirit, tragedy fell grimly across his life. The great wolf-dog of the brazier's, a sour and sinister neighbor whose farm abutted the Tröen farm, slashed the throat of Peer's lovely little daughter Asta. Peer, the father, and Merle, the mother,

[197]

kept their vigil with death. In the silence of their watch, sorrow, in Bojer's phrase, led Peer farther and farther out on the promontory of existence, until he had come to the outermost point, where he faced the ultimate issues of life. He wavered between madness and resignation. But, finally, a spark began glowing in him. "Standing on the ruins of my life," said Peer, "I felt a vast responsibility. Mankind must arise, and be better than the blind powers that order its ways; in the midst of its sorrows it must take heed that the god-like does not die." Faced by what seemed to him the "dead omnipotence" of the universe, Peer determined to do his part in creating the divine on earth.

The spring had been a season of terrible drought. And when at last the people sowed their fields with corn, frost and snow and sleet froze the seed in the ground. The brazier's field was barren. And he could neither beg nor buy seed for its resowing, for, since he had loosed his savage wolf-dog to take the life of little Asta, he had been a hated and harassed man in the parish. The barrenness of the brazier's field beat in upon Peer's spirit. "It won't do us any good, you know," he said to Merle, "to see his bit of field lying bare all summer." And so he stole silently out into the night, that none might know it was he, and sowed the brazier's field with corn. "I went out and sowed corn in my enemy's field," he explained, "that God might exist."

To the ancient drama in which Job suggests that friends should be kind to a despairing man to prevent his losing faith in the Almighty, and to the modern tale in which Peer Tröen says that he sowed his enemy's field with corn in order that God might exist, all the current circumstances of American life add their weight in support of the contention that the spiritual life of men and nations is profoundly affected by the secular life in which its values must find living expression.

The future of religion on this continent depends less upon the explanations of professors and the exhortations of parsons than upon the kind of political, social, and economic life we contrive to create and to maintain. In the creation and maintenance of a valid national life, we are, therefore, engaged in an enterprise in which secular and spiritual interests meet and merge.

VIII

NATIONALISM AMUCK

AT THE moment the economic relations of the world are paralyzed by a baffling paradox. While the processes of the world's life grow daily more international, the policies of the world's governments grow daily more national.

Credit, contract, capital, and corporate organization, in their modern forms, rapid transportation, instantaneous communication, and all the varied media through which the forces of science, technology, and power production now express themselves and upon which they depend for a full and free functioning are inherently the tools of a world civilization. They are out of place in a parochial economy. And yet, with singular unanimity, the major governments of the world are to-day turning to a neo-tribalism of policy.

If, as the philosophers of resurgent nationalism insist that it is, this is more than a transient by-product of the economic flux and emotional fanaticism of a passing phase of stress, it confronts us with the unavoidable necessity of deciding whether, as a matter of permanent policy, we are to walk the ways of a realistic internationalism, in so far as the policies of other peoples will permit, or go frankly in for the economic monasticism of the nationalists.

It is difficult for anyone not at the center of government to speak with a sure judgment on this issue. The political and economic foreign policies of the United States do not operate in a vacuum. They cannot but be profoundly influenced by policy elsewhere in the world. And, at any given moment, a hundred and one detailed difficulties, known only to those in actual charge of diplomatic negotiations, may block the immediate application of what may seem, from some observation post outside the government, the obviously statesman-like policy. The foreign policy of a major government cannot be run in detail from the bleachers.

On the other hand, the peace of the people and the prosperity of the enterprise of the United States are deeply involved in the currently increasing nationalism of political policy alongside an increasing internationalism of economic interest. So deeply involved, in fact, that no audit of the American outlook can ignore the ultimate implications of an intensified nationalism in an age whose driving forces of science, technology, and power production are straining against the political frontiers and trade barriers that stand as hurdles to the energies of economic modernism. I must, therefore, attempt an analysis of the growing capitulation of contemporary governments to the philosophy of exclusive economic nationalism, autarchy, or the self-contained nation, as this trend is variously defined.

Paradoxically enough, a multitude of forces were making for a new birth of nationalism throughout Europe in the decade following the close of a war that had, in theory at least, been fought to promote a productive internationalism. The staggering weight of war debts and reparations. The urgent need of rebuilding ruined areas and reconstructing the disrupted mechanisms of normal production and distribution. The chaos that came on the heels of the relaxation of the strong governmental controls which, for the duration of the war, had largely adjourned private concerns in the interest of a public cause. The political impatience and social radicalism of disillusioned veterans who failed to find, upon their return from the trenches, the promised lands that were to be fit for heroes. The sweep of self-determination across a Europe that stood more in need of firmer integration than of further division. The new volume and the new variety of production which, stimulated by the war in all countries, disrupted the old patterns of world trade. The hangover of fear for wars to come, which no preventive device fashioned at Paris had allayed, and the consequent determination to become as self-sufficient as possible before war should come again. And so on through a disheartening catalogue.

These and like problems, plights, and passions combined to drive the thought of the European nations inward as they faced the bewildering uncertainties of the post-war period. There was much activity looking toward new formulas for intergovernmental cooperation, and the inherently transnational interests of European industry carried on conferences and effected combines which, in significant instances, ignored the frontiers of race and politics. But these were eddies. The main stream was carrying all of Europe toward nationalism of a new and intensified sort.

In the countries which, like England and France, have stuck most closely to their established traditions of government, this new nationalism has expressed itself mainly in restrictive tariff and trade legislation and intermittent buy-at-home crusades. In the countries which, like Russia and Italy and Germany, have broken more decisively with their pre-war political traditions, this new nationalism has been given the emotional content of a secular religion, invested with ritualism and regalia, and subjected to the iron discipline of the drill ground.

Governments of this latter sort have consciously chosen this new and extreme nationalism as a way of life for their peoples, but the nations which have made no such open decision have nevertheless been caught in a relentless drift toward a like philosophy. It is becoming more and more apparent that, in the absence of some new and at the moment unindicated move, the United States will be increasingly driven in the direction of an extreme economic nationalism.

I do not mean that we shall deliberately build a Chinese Wall about our enterprise. It will, in all probability, be more like the rail fences I knew as a boy in Missouri. There will be loose rails that can be lifted so that the fence can, for the moment, be more easily vaulted. There will be sections of the fence missing here and there, and through these openings we shall attempt modest forays into foreign trade fields. As things are now set, however, we shall be forced in the general direction of an economic nationalism more exclusive than any we have yet known.

Any such development, that largely deletes world trade from the American economic picture, will involve drastic readjustments in the organization, capitalization, and operation of most of our major enterprises in business, industry, and agriculture, will harass our financiers with problems more vexatious than they have yet faced, and will make inevitable a severity and scope of internal regimentation from Washington which, barring some miraculous change in the national temper, will prove intolerable to Americans generally.

That practical difficulties without precedent today stand in the way of an active resumption of world trade as we knew it in pre-war and early post-war days is obvious. Some of these difficulties are temporary in nature, incident to the general disruption the war worked in the world's enterprise, and will ultimately disappear as the world makes its half-century climb back to normal. Such difficulties as are thus temporary, and do not reflect a permanent change in the design and direction of world trade, must be dealt with as the best day-to-day judgment of men at the centers of political and economic power may direct. They present issues of strategy upon which public opinion is not and cannot be equipped to pass.

That all of the difficulties surrounding world trade are not temporary, but represent permanent changes in the import and export problems of the world, is equally obvious. The real question, therefore, is whether the basic forces of science, technology, and power production, through the process of industrialization they have set going, have so altered the economic activities, interests, and relations of the varied nations as to make necessary some radically new deal in world trade relations that shall permanently minimize the element of interchange and permanently magnify the element of isolation. On this question there is both the need and the possibility of an informed public opinion to affect the broad trend of American policy. This is a matter too basic to be left to the uncertain mercies of political opportunism or economic jockeying.

There are three sources of opinion and interest respecting world relations that must be taken into account in any examination of the forces now making for exclusive nationalism among the Western nations: (1) The political opportunists who conceive the administration of foreign relations as a form of horse-trading in which principles are to be improvised from day to day to meet shifting pressures, and who incline to whatever foreign policy promises to prove most popular with their local constituents; (2) the chauvinists who, from an emotional bias, are so jealously and belligerently national that they bristle at the slightest suggestion of concession that might smooth the working of the world's life, and who, from an economic bias, seek to block any tariff or trade policy, no matter how salutary it may be for the people as a whole, if it threatens to take from them any traditionally protected privilege; and (3) the philosophers of the new nationalism who are convinced that the progressive industrialization of the world has rendered the old policies of interchange obsolete and that a wholly new concept of domestic economy and foreign trade is imperative.

It is idle to waste words on the political opportunists and the chauvinists. They are little moved by reason. The springs of their action are more elemental. The philosophers of the new nationalism are in a different category. Their pleas spring from a sincere attempt to reconsider the problem of world trade in the light of the changes induced in the world's economic life by the forces of science, technology, and power production, with the aftermath of the war as a correlative but not controlling factor. They take note of the special circumstance of a world in which a near-universal war has given to all the major nations a volume and variety of production it had not occurred to them to attempt before. They take note of the general circumstance attending the end of an era in which many hitherto undeveloped territories have, in the process of being exploited by the industrialized nations, become themselves industrialized, and so are now in some measure competitors where once they were safety-valves of these older industrialized nations. And they reckon also with the fact that all of the major nations, if they have not actually reached, are at least potentially in position to move rapidly toward a magnitude of output that will make the problem of profitable market-outlets increasingly difficult.

The new nationalists fall roughly into two contingents, the idealists and the strategists. These two contingents agree on the arguments for an intensified nationalism, but the strategists are less concerned than the idealists with the elaboration of a philosophy of economic nationalism as an inherently sound basis for world relations quite apart from the difficulties that currently hamper world trade. In the spirit of practical politics, the strategists are primarily concerned to find a way of escape from the tight corner in which economic America now finds itself. The idealists are moving toward a new theory of international relations they think desirable. The strategists are moving away from an old practice of international relations they think dangerous.

The idealists, to whom economic nationalism is a desirable philosophy of world relations apart from the difficulties now surrounding world trade, insist that foreign trade should be judged by its impact upon the living standards of the consuming majority rather than by its impact upon the profits of the exporting minority of the American people. World trade should not, in their judgment, be looked upon as a field from which to reap large profits, but should be used only as a means of securing for ourselves goods, services, and cultural contacts we could not otherwise enjoy. We should not, they say, export any more of our output than may be necessary to pay for these goods, services, and cultural contacts which we could not secure save through such exchange. They advise, in short, that we put our trade with the rest of the world essentially on a barter basis. A temporary excess of exports over imports should, they suggest, be allowed to discharge debts that may, from time to time, be owed to other nations. This exception has but slight relevance for us, however, since we are now and are likely to remain for a long run of decades a creditor nation.

Upon these simple but sweeping premises the more idealistic of the new nationalists erect their philosophy of a balanced economy for the United States. And they think that a balanced economy of this sort, under which exports and imports are made exact offsets one to the other, would, if we alone adopted it, bear important fruits for us internally, and, if generally adopted by the nations of the world, would bear important fruits internationally.

Internally, they think, it would drive us to a development of our home market which, for all our fanfare of advertising and hectic drives of high-pressure salesmanship, we have grossly neglected. We have, in their judgment, spent more time courting than cultivating our home market. If we forgot world trade as a material source of profit, however, we would, they say, be compelled to expand the purchasing power of our army of small earners and, in every other available way, to work out domestic policies that would enable us to put to effective use here at home the total output of our enterprise, aside from what we might barter with other nations or send abroad in payment of debt. And this, if realized, they rightly think, would mean an economic advantage to the producers as well as a social advantage to the people as a whole.

Internationally, they think, the philosophy of a balanced economy generally adopted would forever eliminate the race for markets, which has been one of the most active causes of war, and the permanent peace of the world would be brought nearer to realization. In other words, they see a world regime of relatively self-contained nationalisms making for peace rather than war.

[209]

The philosophy of economic nationalism is, they think, in harmony with historic inevitability. It reflects what is due to happen. They see the British Empire moving toward a self-contained commonwealth of self-governing peoples. They see Russia in the march of nations moving toward self-containment. As this process goes on, they think that the varied nations of Europe, once they see that they cannot depend upon the economic disunity of the rest of the world, will iron out their European difficulties and will act in unity to achieve a self-contained Europe. Asia, they think, will follow suit, with a self-contained East as the end result. Maybe a self-contained America, made up of the United States and the countries of Central and South America, will be added to the picture. And then, they think, some three or four large aggregations of nations, each having planned its domestic life intelligently, will work out an orderly system of interchange of goods and service on the basis of use rather than profit, a system of world trade that will have in it none of the old cutthroat competition that has so long kept the world in the shadow of war.

The idealistic new nationalists are neither opportunists nor chauvinists. They are seeking, in all sincerity, the establishment of rational relationships between the nations of the world, each of which has organized its enterprise as nearly as possible on a basis of self-containment, and they think that the nations cannot severally plan their

domestic economies adequately without first building something of a wall about their enterprise.

The new nationalists who are primarily interested, not in world policy, but in a strategy of
survival and success for American enterprise put
their case more simply.

The world, they say, is moving relentlessly
toward universal industrialization. It is only a
question of time until there will be no backward
and undeveloped territories to serve as outlets for
the surplus capital and surplus goods of the industrialized nations. The phase of industrial expansion into outlying areas which made the nineteenth
a century tingling with adventure slows down to its
close. The trade of the future, they say, must be,
not between industrial and non-industrial countries, not between developed and undeveloped
countries, but between highly industrialized countries themselves.

This would not be a particularly menacing
prospect if the nations followed the traditional idea
of national specialization, with each nation producing the particular things that place and people best
fitted it to produce. But this, they say, is not the
outlook. The war forced all the participating
nations to go as far toward economic self-sufficiency
as possible, but, even without the war, the advance
of industrialization would have swelled the volume
and widened the variety of production in all the
major nations, a little more slowly, it may be, but
none the less surely. Can nations like England,

France, Germany, Italy, Japan, Belgium, Czecho-slovakia, and the United States live by taking in each other's washing, they ask, after each has equipped itself to do essentially the same sort of washing?

And we Americans, they say, have no permanent advantage, either of folk or of facilities, in modern industrial enterprise because less skill and briefer apprenticeship are required of workmen in mass-production industries than were required of the workmen in the shops of the older and smaller scale machine industries. A lower level of capacity can, in consequence, be called upon to man the mass-production factories of the nations that are now entering fully into industrial competition with us. Nation after nation that we have not hereto-fore regarded seriously as industrial rivals will become serious rivals, it is suggested, as mass-production methods enable them to use in their industries great masses of workmen heretofore thought by us to be unfitted, both by their temper-ament and by their tradition, to service in modern industry. The most we can say, it is contended, is that we have a head start on the rest of the world in this business of mass production.

The upshot of all this, the nationalists concerned with our economic strategy say, is that we, along with the other industrial nations, must, in large measure bid goodbye to foreign trade and con-centrate our attention on the home market.

How valid is all this? It must be admitted that the case for autarchy or a self-contained nationalism as thus stated is, on the surface, not only plausible, but convincing. It does not seem to me, however, to stand a closer scrutiny. Certain of the contentions upon which the case rests raise obvious questions.

For one thing, industrialization has far from covered the world to the extent that the average American is likely to infer from the arguments of the nationalists when they suggest that industrialization has brought the era of an active world trade measurably to an end. Even at this late date it is but a minority of the world's population that is involved in modern industrialism. Peasantry is still the way of life for a very large part of modern humanity. Little Japan has, indeed, industrialized herself. And Africa and the Far East have seen the small beginnings of industrialization. Very small, indeed, as evidenced by the fact that but little more than seven-tenths of one per cent of the swarming population of India is actively involved in the enterprises of manufacture and transportation in the industrialized sense in which we pursue them. Industrialization has touched China even less, and Africa still less.

And this industrialization of the still unindustrialized areas of the globe is not likely to move with the airplane speed the arguments of the nationalists seem to suggest by indirection. Speedy industrialization requires the existence of accumulated capital, technical competence, natural resources that are adequate and readily available, and the prompt spreading of buying power through wages to the masses to an extent that will provide an assured consumer market for the output of the new productive capacity created by industrialization. It is not a simple matter to walk into an India, with its 348,000,000 people, or into a China, with its 444,000,000 people, the vast majority of whom are living on the lowest poverty level, whose tastes are tastes schooled in the school of near-starvation, and in whose brains and hands little of technical competence exists, and, by sending money and machines and a flying squadron of experts into the land, effect an industrialization of the national enterprise.

The thing can be done, of course, and the doing of it would bring two inestimable boons. It would give to the business, industry, and finance of the world a job which, in challenge and profit, would make the expansive enterprise of the nineteenth century seem the play of amateurs. And it would at last put at the service of the whole of mankind those forces of science, technology, and power production which to-day a minority of mankind finds so distressingly productive that it can think of nothing better than to curb them, either negatively by tolerating cyclic crises or positively by restrictive legislation. The job is not impossible. The vast unindustrialized areas of the world can be industrialized, and the now stalled energies of this power age kept busy at full tilt for more than the lifetime of any of us now living, but this cannot be done, save over the slow and painful road of plodding generations, as long as the madness of exclusive nationalism dominates world policy.

The industrialization of the still unindustrialized areas of the world can be done, within a range of time short enough to prevent the collapse and release the locked energies of the power economy of the industrialized nations, only through a revised policy of world relations under which the responsible leaderships of all countries, in the light of a truly intelligent self-interest, tackle the economic development of the world as a common problem, and tackle it in terms of economic policies that have been made to fit the nature and need of enterprise in an age of science, technology, and power production.

Then, too, it is not true, as the casual reader might be led to think from some of the literature of the new nationalism, that industrialization *ipso facto* means a drastic lessening of the imports of the industrialized nation. It may well alter the nature of the imports. It need not shrink them. It may greatly expand them. An Oriental country like India, let us say, becomes industrialized. It goes in for mass production in the American manner. It will, in consequence, need to import less and less of the kind of manufactured goods it has learned itself to make in quantity. But the very process of production that reduces imports of this nature will create and spread among the people new wealth with which they may satisfy their demand for imports of a different nature. Every lift that industrialization can make in the living standards of peoples now unindustrialized or little industrialized means potentially an expansion rather than a constriction of markets for other producing nations. If constriction of total imports occurs, the root-cause of the constriction is likely to be found elsewhere than in the fact of industrialization.

To turn to another contention advanced by the new nationalists, I question the assumption that we have no fundamental advantage in the field of modernized power production other than a head start on the rest of the world. At least I question the assumption upon which this assumption rests. There is only temporary truth to the assertion that the development of power production puts most jobs wholly within the capacity zone of a lower and lower grade of labor. However regrettable it may be on this or that social count, the ultimate capacity requirements of power production will be the opposite. Modernized power production moves relentlessly in the direction of fewer workers with higher capacity, not in the direction of more workers with lower capacity.

Lewis Mumford, in his *Technics and Civilization*, subjects to searching analysis that complete automatism toward which our modern system of power production is moving. " . . . the worker, instead of being a source of work, becomes an observer and regulator of the performance of the machines, a supervisor of production rather than an active agent," he says. "Indeed the direct control of the local worker is the same in principle as the remote control of the management itself, supervising, through reports and charts, the flow of power and goods through the entire plant. The qualities the new worker needs are alertness, responsiveness, an intelligent grasp of the operative parts; in short, he must be an all-round mechanic rather than a specialized hand."

This is the ultimate labor demand that an industrialism of modernized power production will make. In temperament, in tradition, and in training, we are equipped to meet this demand with as prompt adequacy as any, and with prompter adequacy than most, of the peoples alike of the West and of the East. Mass production has not suddenly and will not swiftly recruit for industrial production throughout the world vast masses of workers whose temperament, tradition, and training have set their lives to a different technique and a different tempo. Barring a nullification of our productive genius through economic and political blundering, we can hold the head start we have.

And, finally, the contention of the new nationalists that we must, in large measure, bid goodbye to foreign trade and concentrate on the home market has wider implications than meet the eye.

The United States, it may be at once admitted, is more nearly in position to embark upon a policy of self-contained nationalism than any other of the major nations. It has a vast expanse of territory, politically unified, commercially unhampered by internal tariff barriers, containing unusually varied sources of power, richly stocked with natural resources as a sustaining diet for its machines, and populated by 125,000,000 customers for the output of its power economy. If any nation can organize its enterprise in relative disregard of the rest of the world it is the United States.

No single nation of Europe is in like position, although Russia approximates it, with her range of territory, population, and resources. If all of Europe were an ethnic and political unity, not lacerated as now by sharp frontiers and separative trade barriers, a pan-European self-sufficiency would approach feasibility. As it is, however, self-sufficiency is a flying goal that none of the separate nations of Europe may hope to reach.

Any persistent attempt to organize the national economies of Europe on a basis of self-sufficiency will result in an increasingly unstable and wasteful Europe. Modernized power production cannot make the fruits of its efficiency socially available without a largeness of operative scale and market outlet that none of the nations of Europe can alone provide. This holds true for even the large nations of Europe. It becomes doubly true for the smaller nations. Sound business planning would never attempt to establish for the limited market of a small country the total range of modern manufactures. It would stick to industries that can be operated efficiently on a small scale, venturing into forms of production that, by their very nature, require largeness of operative scale only if there was a dependable competitive chance to capture the requisite amount of export trade. The sweep of economic nationalism to date in Europe has underwritten the soundness of these contentions.

The cost of living has been lifted and the standard of living lowered for millions of Europeans by the fact that, in the struggle for self-sufficiency, so many of the smaller nations have set up grossly uneconomic industries and have, in consequence, charged for certain goods prices out of all reasonable relation to what the cost of their production would have been in industries established by business planning instead of political hysteria.

I am aware, of course, that not all of this uneconomic industrial development in the lesser and larger nations of Europe has been prompted by a post-war drive for self-sufficiency. Much of it has been due to the post-war tenacity of war-created enterprises which should never have been considered other than emergency enterprises. Industries, improvised during the war to serve an abnormal situation in which the normal principles of sound business planning and operation had to be disregarded, instead of demobilizing at the end of the war, settled down as permanent industries and began bombarding their governments for tariff protection against better planned, better placed, and better prosecuted enterprises elsewhere. These, however, quite as effectively as industries deliberately created for the purpose, illustrate the inefficiency, waste, and high-cost production that must inevitably result from forced attempts to attain self-sufficiency in areas not basically equipped for a complete economic life.

Even if a self-contained United States were within range of easy achievement, the European situation is such that a permanent commitment of the nations generally to an intensified economic nationalism could not but result in an inefficient, wasteful, and unstable world in which the modernist forces of science, technology, and power production would be estopped from lowering the cost and lifting the standard of living for the human race. It seems to me naive in the extreme to suppose that the United States, for all its resources and resourcefulness, could escape influence from the political distraction, economic disruption, and social dishevelment that would, under such circumstances, become the chronic condition of European life.

It is too late in the long evolutionary climb of productive method for nationalism of this sort. The techniques of power production cannot be employed in rabbit warrens. They need room and range. And the nations of Europe cannot separately furnish this room and range. If we now attempt to crowd the genii of science, technology, and power into the bottle of nationalism, we may but break the bottle.

We could, as I have said, more nearly than any other nation, approach economic self-sufficiency. This is not to say that we could reach it or closely approach it without paying a very heavy price in internal readjustment and regimentation. It is true that we have within our own borders most, but by no means all, of the essentials of economic life, but this does not make us a self-contained nation, for the simple reason that, wisely or unwisely, on the foundation of our admittedly magnificent resources, we have so organized, so capitalized, and so elaborated the productive mechanism of most of our major enterprises of business, industry, and agriculture that these enterprises cannot produce with maximum effectiveness for the domestic market unless concurrently they can sell in foreign markets such surplus as they, from time to time, find themselves geared to produce. We cannot move far in the direction of economic exclusiveness, therefore, without facing the necessity of sweeping readjustment and stringent regimentation of the whole private enterprise of the nation.

The new nationalists insist that, since foreign trade has never absorbed more than from 6 to 10 per cent of our total production, its importance to our economic well-being has been grossly overestimated. This contention illustrates the danger of generalizing too readily from statistical averages. It is true that for the last thirty or more years our total exports have represented only about 6 to 10 per cent of our total production. These aggregate figures, however, give little guidance to our judgment on the relation of foreign trade to the effective functioning of our domestic economy. Unless we burrow under and break down these production and export totals into their several commodity elements, we do not get an accurate sense of the significance of exports to the national life. If an export total running to but 10 per cent of the national production meant that every major product of American enterprise found 90 per cent of its market in the United States, we could, as far as the sales end of our enterprise was concerned, build a wall around ourselves, let the rest of the world stew in its own juice, and build within our own borders a satisfactory and viable economic life. That this is not the case is clear from an examination of some of the factors that enter into the aggregate 10 per cent of our national production that has normally been sold abroad.

In 1929, a climactic point in the development of our productive facilities, more than 54 per cent of American cotton was sold abroad, more than 41 per cent of American leaf tobacco, nearly 40 per cent of American kerosene, over 40 per cent of American typewriters, about 36 per cent of American copper, nearly 34 per cent of American lard, about 31 per cent of American lubricating oil, over

29 per cent of American printing machinery, about 28 per cent of American sewing machines, and more than 23 per cent of American farm machinery.

The extent to which these ten representative products have been severally dependent upon export outlets indicates that the drastic diminution or discontinuance of foreign trade involves impacts upon American enterprise far more serious than an aggregate 10 per cent of our total production would suggest. The fact is that, short of a revolutionary reorganization of American business, industry, and agriculture, we shall remain, as we are, importantly dependent upon world markets.

Despite much of current opinion to the contrary, every consideration of fact convinces me that the modern world cannot be operated effectively in terms of a series of economic nationalisms, each struggling for the utmost measure of self-sufficiency. The modern world is bound together by the inherently trans-national forces of rapid transportation, swift communication, credit, contract, capital, and corporate organization. We cannot reverse this basic fact by transient ventures in swashbuckling nationalism. Ultimately an integrated world policy must dominate world trade relations. Such policy seems impossible of prompt achievement at the moment, but it is one of the major obligations the time puts upon us to surmount rather than surrender to the difficulties that to-day tie statesmanship to the parish pump the world around.

I am aware that many frankly regard anything other than a severely restricted nationalism of economic enterprise as impossible. The distinguished Dean of the Graduate School of Business Administration of Harvard University, Mr. Donham, in his *Business Looks at the Unforeseen*, expresses with complete candor this skepticism of any policy beyond economic nationalism.

"The truth is," he writes, "that the effective organization of the world on the basis of constantly expanding interdependence is beyond human intelligence. Too many cultures clash at too many points. Too many facts, hopelessly beyond both intellectual and practical mastery, prevent mutual understanding. Too many local economic and social problems require solutions not consonant with any general plan directed at the best average solution for the total population of the globe. Too great differences in standards of living exist in different parts of the world. The road to peace by the accentuation of mutual interdependence is hopeless. The only hope lies in the lessening of points of conflict so that in our remaining points of contact we may attain mutual understanding."

Unless I am far afield in judgment, this is not so much realism as it is a running away from the problem. It is not necessary thus to run up the white flag of surrender in the face of modern complexity. This running away from complexity is evident in many contemporary fields other than

[224]

foreign policy. It is one of the major weaknesses of modern intelligence.

The conviction that the problem of modern interdependence is beyond our power of mastery is a reflection in the field of affairs of a conviction that has lately prevailed in the field of knowledge. It has been widely assumed that knowledge was once simple enough for mastery, but has, in our time, become complex beyond the comprehension of any single mind, that the synoptic grasp of an Aristotle or a Bacon is no longer possible, and that the best we can do is to settle down to the intellectual truck-farming of tiny plots of specialization. This is intellectual defeatism on the part of scholars who, scared by the dust storms of data that whirl ceaselessly across their path, have surrendered in the face of the results of their own research, as the new nationalists are surrendering in the face of the complexity brought to the world's affairs by the modernist forces of science, technology, and power production. In the field of knowledge, we have seemed to say that we could know nothing because we know so much, and now, in the field of affairs, it is suggested that we can do nothing because we have equipped ourselves to do so much.

The fact is that no single mind was ever able to master all of human knowledge or bring all of the recalcitrant forces of human society to heel. Alike in the field of scholarship and in the field of statesmanship, it has always been a question of the capacity of leadership to see, state, and secure adherence to essential meanings that have run like binding threads through the knowledge or the affairs of a time. And this is quite as possible to-day as at any time in recorded history. I could name a half dozen Americans who have quite as understanding grasp of the major implications of modern knowledge as Aristotle and Bacon had of the knowledge of their times. And it is, I think, nothing but an unconscious rationalization of our frightened retreat from reality that leads us to assume that the complexities of world relations are now beyond practical mastery.

I am aware that American statesmanship must, in this singularly disorganized phase of the world's life, stand stubborn guard over American interests. I have no desire to see the United States set irresponsibly out as a gullible Sir Galahad in a world of Robin Hoods. I am aware that the nature and volume of world trade have changed radically in the post-war period as nation after nation has enlarged its production of commodities that formerly bulked large in our export trade.

But, for all this, I am convinced that the current swing toward self-contained nationalism is a venture in madness. If unchecked, it will mean the retreat of the civilized modern to primitive tribalism. It will enforce revolutionary readjustments in the organization, capitalization, and operation of all our major enterprises, It will make necessary a

sweeping political regimentation of business, industry, and agriculture that is repugnant to the
American spirit. It will spell the doom of commer-
cial agriculture on this continent, and drive the
American farmer to the status of the peasant, with
a standard of living higher, perhaps, than the hard
lot of the European peasant, but with the subsistence income that marks the peasant nevertheless.
It will mean that a baffled statesmanship the world
around is setting out to liquidate the age of plenty
and lead mankind back to an age of scarcity.

I have purposely put the case against economic
nationalism extremely, because the case for economic nationalism has been put extremely. I do
not mean merely to echo the old cry of the economic
imperialist. I have no desire to see revived the
racketeering practices that attended the older
imperialistic exploitation of world markets and
backward territories. I am aware that the export
of capital and goods to undeveloped areas has
rounded out a pioneer phase, and that the nature
of the problem has changed. I agree with many
of the contentions of the philosophers of the new
nationalism, despite my disagreement with their
major conclusion. I agree that foreign trade, like
domestic industry, must increasingly be judged by
its impact upon the lives of the millions. I agree
that the sporadic and unsystematized exploitative
expansion of the nineteenth century has left us
with important problems of assimilation and con-
solidation that we have too long neglected. And

I am acutely aware of the innumerable non-economic factors that to-day divide the peoples of the world.

None of these considerations, however, indicate to me, as they seem to indicate to some observers, that industrial and agricultural expansion has come virtually to a dead end. Facts without number indicate to me the contrary. As I stated at the outset, in the sense of latent but clearly feasible capacity, we are in an economy of plenty, but, in no true sense, are we in a surplus economy. Our congested surpluses are false surpluses. They stand in mockery of manifest human need. Both internally and internationally, a vast expansion of industrial and agricultural output waits only the requisite readjustments in economic policy that will release the full productivity of the power age.

Nor do these considerations suggest to me, as they seem to suggest to some observers, either the desirability or the inevitability of extreme economic nationalism. They are simply new and, let us admit, stubborn factors that must be taken intelligently into account in that realistic modernization of the economic policies and trade relations of the world, the necessity of which they vividly enforce.

"No one who visits Hereford Cathedral can fail to be struck by the marvellous *Mappa Mundi* of Richard de Haldingham, which adorns the south choir aisle," said F. J. C. Hearnshaw, in a lecture on *Nicolo Machiavelli* at King's College, University of London, some years ago. "It represents the theological conception of the world at the close of the thirteenth century. The habitable earth which it portrays is flat and circular, like a rimless plate, surrounded by a narrow fringe of ocean. At the center of the circle stands Jerusalem; at the extreme east the Garden of Eden; midway between the two the Tower of Babel. Round the margin at different points are situated such places as the peninsula in which Gog and Magog were interned by Alexander the Great, the Earthly Paradise discovered by St. Brandan, and the British Isles. On various otherwise unoccupied spots in Asia and Africa are to be found such interesting curiosities as the kingdom of Prester John, the realm of the Amazons, the granaries of Joseph, and the land of the Sciapodes, those fascinating one-legged folk whose solitary foot was so large and adaptable that it not only carried them about with incredible celerity, but also served them when they rested as a shelter from the tropical sun."

We may safely assume with Mr. Hearnshaw that not even in the thirteenth century did it ever occur to any master mariner to set sail with this *Mappa Mundi* as his guide, and that had he so sailed his voyage would have ended in speedy and irretrievable disaster.

"At the very time, however," said Mr. Hearnshaw, "when the pious prebendary of Haldingham was concocting from the Scriptures and the mythologies this fantastic travesty of the world as it actually exists, Italian seamen, particularly those of Venice and Genoa, on the basis of careful observation and repeated experiment, were constructing for practical purposes *portolani*, or mariners' charts, which give an amazingly accurate and minute representation of that Mediterranean basin wherein the main maritime commerce of the Middle Ages was concentrated."

The extreme economic nationalists are the Richard de Haldinghams of contemporary world economics. They have constructed an economic *Mappa Mundi* that does not reflect reality. Another generation may find their chart of world relations on the wall of some museum, as Richard de Haldingham's fantasy now hangs in Hereford Cathedral. If political leadership will but keep its head, resist the seductive arguments of the economic nationalists, and hold the field open for intelligent experimentation, practical business genius, disciplined by these lean years of vanished exports and driven to think in world terms, may construct for us economic *portolani* by which it will again be possible to navigate the now drying channels of world trade.

IX

THE ALTERNATIVE TO REVOLUTION

ONE thing should by now be clear to all literate Americans, namely, that the temper of the crowd and the turn of affairs economic have combined to create a situation in which beating the tom-tom for obsolete traditions of politics and economics can neither satisfy the mass mind nor bring recovery and stabilization to our enterprise.

The psychological forces playing upon our problem are more than the limited forces of a local situation. We are not hermetically sealed against what is happening elsewhere in the world. The subtle disintegration or willing surrender of self-government, the repudiation of freedom, the subordination of the individual, the exaltation of the state, the brutalizing advance of a berserker nationalism, the propagandist perversion of education, the waning of faith in science as a force for human emancipation, the popular desertion of the altars of religion and the political determination to make the church a press agent of national aims, the exacerbation of class conflict, and the seductive influence of fatigue-poisoned leaderships that have tired of trying to master the dynamic forces of modernism and are content to huddle about the cooling embers of a curbed industrialism and a constricted agriculture, all these, here or there evident in larger or lesser measure throughout the kaleidoscopic change that races through Western life and enterprise, are forces affecting the emotional climate in which the American process of readjustment must function.

The maladjustments we must meet with measures of correction are more than the temporary throwing out of gear of an otherwise fully modernized machine. The major perplexities that disturb the political and economic leadership of the United States are all rooted in three basic difficulties which the whole of the industrialized world has had to face: (1) The but thinly veiled breakdown of the world's financial system, due to the fact that the world's credit and currency system has not been kept wisely adjusted to the changing needs of the world's economic enterprise; (2) the revolutionary changes that science, technology, and power have effected in the world's industrial system, with the result that fewer and fewer workers in less and less time can produce more than the world's population can buy, with its present purchasing power, or use, with its present margin of leisure; and (3) the strange revival, since the war, of a stubborn and swashbuckling nationalism that stands in active opposition to an increasing internationalism of economic interest, with the result that the world's political system is making virtually impossible the operation of an effective economic system either within the nations or between the nations. These, it will be seen, are major maladjustments calling for major readjustments that will bring our financial, economic, and political arrangements into harmony with the life processes of an age of plenty.

Events must sooner or later convince even the most reluctant traditionalist that, unless and until we restudy and readjust the financial order, the economic order, and the political order in terms of the new circumstances of this new age of science, technology, and power production, our ventures in political and economic management can be but little more than an irrelevant shadow-boxing in the suburbs of reality.

We are confronted by an unprecedented situation calling for an unprecedented willingness to consider unprecedented policies. Neither an irrational radicalism nor an irrational reaction is tolerable under these circumstances. We shall escape the phase of social disruption, through which so much of mankind has lately passed, only through the exercise of a cool and constructive intelligence that refuses to let its approach to reality be obscured either by the traditions of reaction or by the theories of radicalism.

There are frightened reactionaries who are sure we are drifting into Communism. There are frightened radicals who are sure we are drifting into Fascism. We may, I think, safely take both these fears with a grain of salt. Nations never drift into either Fascism or Communism. Nations go Fascist or Communist, in the open and formal sense of Italian Fascism and Russian Communism, only when the soil is thoroughly prepared for the seed, and when there is behind the Fascist or Communist *Putsch* a capable, clear-headed, closely knit, and rigidly disciplined group able to get its hands quickly on the levers of military and economic power. There is nothing in the American picture to indicate that we have reached such a point. And there is nothing inherent in the situation that need ever lead us to such a pass if we but use our heads.

We are not an easily inflammable people. Even the more moderate movement of American socialism has not made dramatic headway during the last decade. In 1920, Eugene Debs polled more than 200,000 votes in New York State and more than 900,000 votes in the country as a whole. Twelve years later, in 1932, in a time of incredible economic hardship, when the wine of discontent was everywhere in ferment, the able and persuasive Norman Thomas polled only 175,000 votes in New York State and only about 800,000 votes in the country as a whole. I am aware that, in 1932, a large protest vote, that might under more normal circumstances have gone to the Socialist candidate, went to Franklin D. Roosevelt. But that hardly argued a revolt-obsessed people, for what has seemed to some the radicalism of Rooseveltian policies has largely developed since the election. I submit, therefore, that both the low vote of Norman Thomas and the high vote of Franklin D. Roosevelt indicated that we are not an easily inflammable people.

I have consistently refused to be stampeded by the alarmists. I believe that the American philosophy of private enterprise and political liberty, if now corrected in the light of experience and adjusted wisely to the new requirements of an age of plenty, will be functioning after all of us now living have long been dead and the Fascisms and Communisms of the moment have become the relics of dead yesterdays. But the confidence I have that capitalism and democracy will survive is contingent upon our willingness to face fresh problems with fresh minds and to effect, without undue delay, the corrections and readjustments the circumstances of the age demand. Even so stable a people as we will not cling forever to a system which leadership declines to keep in working order.

We still have time to choose between guided reconstruction and unguided revolt. I use the word "revolt" instead of the word "revolution" because there is a basic difference between the two, a distinction that would clarify and invest with greater reality our political and economic debate if we could but keep it in mind. This distinction between revolt and revolution was brilliantly enforced by the great Mazzini in his crusade for the socio-moral invigoration of Italy in the early nineteenth century. It was tellingly dramatized by the Duc de la Rochefoucauld as he stood with King Louis watching the Parisian mob storm the Bastille in 1789.

"This is revolt," cried Louis.

"No, Sire," said Rochefoucauld calmly, "it is revolution."

Revolt was there, of course, but Rochefoucauld was right in reminding Louis that he was watching the profounder fact of revolution in which his people had set deliberately out to readjust the old tools of government, which were obsolete, to the new tasks of government, which were obvious to all save the wilfully blind. And this, as Rochefoucauld knew, was a more fundamental thing than mere revolt. It was a far-reaching process of social readjustment in which revolt might or might not take place.

There can be revolt without revolution. There can be revolution without revolt. The greatest revolutions, in fact, are never marred by revolts. We do not want revolt in the United States. And, unless the American intelligence blindly abdicates, we can face difficulties more drastic than we have yet known without revolt. But, unless we are willing to run the risk of a lapse into social and economic chaos, we cannot avoid revolution, if by revolution we mean what we should mean, namely, evolution under the guidance of an intelligence that is neither enslaved by inflexible tradition nor dragged at the heels of ill-conceived change.

[236]

But it is, perhaps, futile to assume that even so unsubtle a distinction as this between revolt and revolution will become a part of the working apparatus of popular thought. We must assume that, for all practical purposes, revolt and revolution mean the same thing to the average American. Revolution will continue to mean, in the mine run of political discussion, the outright overthrow of an existing order in an orgy of violence. And that we do not want. We cannot prevent change. We can pilot it to productive ends. It is in the development of a temper and technique for the direction of change that we can alone find a permanent alternative to revolution as revolution is popularly understood.

Changes are forever taking place in the life and enterprise of living peoples. When change stops we may know that the genius of a people has gone cold and the stream of its civilization gone stagnant. We cannot escape the fact of change no matter how stubborn our orthodoxies. The problem, as I have said, is not to stop change, but to swing it behind constructive purpose.

If flexible intelligence were always at the helm, this constructive guidance of change would proceed as a matter of course, and for the most part quite outside the political war zone in which radicals and reactionaries fill the air with their charges and counter-charges. Our social institutions, our economic policies, and our political mechanisms would be kept progressively adjusted to the changing

[237]

circumstances that are inseparable from the life and enterprise of a living people. The result would be that a people would never come to dramatic turns in the road where, as a strategy of survival, it had to undertake a wholesale readjustment of its institutions to situations too long neglected by its traditional leadership.

But this, unhappily, is not the way the race has functioned to date. There is always a lag between the swiftly changing life and the slowly changing institutions of a people. And it is this fact of lag that gives rise to the sort of crisis that has frozen the fountains of our enterprise for the last five years.

It is right that there should be some lag. Otherwise our institutions would be in a continuous Saint Vitus dance of change that would make ordered life and productive enterprise impossible. We do not want our institutions to chase down the street after every Pied Piper who has snared a new notion from the cloudland of theory. Most new ideas are wrong. By this I mean that the race is lucky if experience ratifies as true one out of every thousand new theories it evolves. Most of the ideas that have survived the stress and storm of the centuries are right. I mean, of course, ideas that have survived with manifest vitality, not ideas that have merely stayed on as cadavers to poison the intellectual atmosphere. All of which means that we must build our lives, individual and institutional, mainly on ideas the race has hammered out on the anvil of experience. No generation can expect to add more than a little to the wisdom of its ancestors. Data it may add by the ton. The wisdom upon which fundamental policy must rest is a different matter.

A certain degree of social lag is desirable in the interest of continuity and stability. We want our institutions to maintain a protective continuity of tradition. We do not want our schools, churches, economic establishments, and governments taken to pieces every evening at sundown and put together again in some new pattern every morning at sunup. It is important to remember, however, that our institutions must maintain continuity with the future as well as continuity with the past. Otherwise they will some day find themselves suddenly tenantless and dark in the midst of a generation whose allegiance they no longer command. We want our institutions to have stability. Unless the institutions of a people stimulate in it a wholesome sense of permanence and predictability, the life and thought and action of the people itself become unstable and unpredictable. It is important to remember, however, that the stability of our institutions must be the equilibrium of steadied action not of mere inertness. Otherwise they become but so much waste lumber cluttering the social scene.

A certain degree of lag between institutional change and social change is, if I may say it again, imperative if civilization is to be kept a going concern. It is not a matter of deciding whether we shall cling to tradition or cultivate change. Tradition and change are not alternatives. They are two indispensable elements of civilization that it is the business of statesmanship to keep in proper relation. It is when the proper relation between tradition and change is unduly disturbed that civilization dies either in the paralysis of reaction or in the convulsions of revolt.

If we permit the policies and procedures of our institutions, under the lordship of inflexible tradition, to lag too far behind the changes that are taking place in the society they were designed to serve, glaring maladjustments occur. These maladjustments produce a social instability. And this social instability may, at any moment, lead an otherwise patient people blindly to break continuity with the sound as well as the unsound values of the past. This, I fear, is the pass to which we have permitted American affairs to come.

I have not come to this conclusion from reading the inflammatory manifestoes of radical agitators. I have been driven to this conviction by such eminently respectable documents as the report of former President Hoover's Research Committee on Recent Social Trends. It is, I submit, impossible for any literate American to read the two major volumes of this Hoover report, together with the subsidiary volumes that elaborate its findings, without realizing that the American civilization of the current decade, both in its nature and in its

[240]

needs, has become a radically different civilization from the American civilization in terms of which our forefathers determined the major patterns and designed the major institutions of our political, social, and economic life. The resistless forces of science, technology, and power have completely remade the civilization going on outside the walls of our institutions. The problems that this changed and changing civilization is to-day putting to government, to business, to industry, to finance, to the church, to the school, and to the family, as these problems are assembled and analyzed in this Hoover report, are drastically different from the problems that faced us even a generation ago. And the report of this Hoover committee dramatizes, as no document before or since has dramatized, the fatal lag between our old policies and our new problems.

This monumental research in social trends boils down to this. Most of the major patterns and most of the major institutions of our political, social, and economic life were designed in terms of an American civilization in which (1) the scale of enterprise was small, (2) the relationships of life simple, and (3) the tempo of affairs slow. But now these institutions must function in and attempt to serve an American civilization in which (1) the scale of enterprise is no longer small, but vast, (2) the relationships of life are no longer simple, but complex, and (3) the tempo of affairs no longer slow, but swift.

The living forces of the new American civilization are straining against the obsolete and obsolescent features of the old American institutions. And the overshadowing problem of this generation is to keep the response of our institutions to the surge of social change reflected in this Hoover report a guided reconstruction unmarred by revolt. Nothing save a flexible intelligence, mediating wisely between the forces of tradition and the forces of change, can possibly insure this result.

The question is not what we should think about some hypothetical "revolt" that the bogey-makers picture as stealing upon us unawares like a thief in the night. The question is what we purpose to do about the actual "revolution" through which the United States has, for some time, been passing, the revolution induced by the forces of science, technology, and power, the revolution so adequately reported and so ably documented by this Research Committee on Recent Social Trends.

The political literature of England has thrown up two immortal pronouncements, rich in statesmanlike guidance to a people, like ourselves, caught in the swirl of a rapidly changing civilization. One of these pronouncements is from John Stuart Mill, the other from Viscount Morley.

"The future of mankind will be gravely imperiled," said John Stuart Mill, "if great questions are left to be fought out between ignorant change and ignorant opposition to change."

"Great economic and social forces flow with tidal sweep over communities only half conscious of that which is befalling them," said Viscount Morley. "Wise statesmen are those who foresee what time is thus bringing, and try to shape institutions and to mould men's thought and purpose in accordance with the change that is silently surrounding them."

These two pronouncements might, with profit, be printed on the title pages of the campaign textbooks of both the Democratic and Republican parties. For it is this emancipation from inflexible tradition and this exercise of flexible intelligence, expressed and exemplified by the John Stuart Mills and the Viscount Morleys, that constitute the most crying need of this distraught time.

The forces of change now so manifestly operative in American affairs may be dammed up by inflexible tradition until they break the dikes with a rush of revolutionary energy or they may be directed by flexible intelligence into a process of political, social, and economic readjustment that will stabilize and invest with fresh significance the national future. In either case, the America of to-morrow will be materially different from the America of yesterday's textbook or to-day's newspaper. And what that America will be like will depend upon whether the forces of inflexible tradition or the forces of flexible intelligence direct our affairs in the days immediately ahead.

We are not, as I have said, an easily inflammable people. I have confidence in the corporate capacity of the American millions, under responsible leadership, to control their own destiny through the peaceful processes of intelligence. But, whatever our reckoning of the probabilities may be, it is but the part of wisdom to face, without wilful self-delusion, the alternative possibilities.

If inflexible tradition controls, we shall inevitably go the way that peoples have always gone when they have lost the capacity or lacked the will intelligently to adjust themselves and their institutions to new circumstances, either falling victim to the subversive forces of revolt, or selling ourselves into slavery to the regimenting forces of dictatorship. The dictatorship might retain the patter and maintain the pretense of reliance upon democratic procedure and be none the less a dictatorship. If we should go the way of revolution, we would be gambling with vast uncertainties, for of all the revolutionary concepts now in the field, from Fascism to Communism, none, in my judgment, offers a tithe of the possibilities of enriched and stabilized life for the millions that lie latent in the American tradition of private enterprise and political liberty. If we should go the way of dictatorship, we would suffer the tragic loss of all those priceless values of liberty, alike in government and in enterprise, without which we might be a nation of contented slaves but never a nation of creative freemen. And thus the forces of tradition would bring about, as a result of their inflexibility, the destruction of the very values they pretended to defend.

If flexible intelligence controls, we shall carefully but courageously adapt the traditional policies and mechanisms of our life and enterprise to the new circumstances of this new age of science, technology, power production, and the political sovereignty of the masses. Some of the things we shall do, if flexible intelligence controls, are clearly indicated.

We shall revise the procedures but remain unreservedly loyal to the principles of democratic self-government.

We shall defend, at whatever cost, alike in government and in enterprise, the utmost freedom consistent with the complex interdependence of modern life.

We shall call upon every resource of ingenuity that is ours to release the full productive energies of the power age that they may lower the cost and lift the standard of living for the masses.

We shall refuse to believe, unless better proof of the necessity than has yet been offered appears, that it is statesmanlike to throw the brakes on our capacity to produce goods and wealth which millions of Americans so manifestly need.

We shall bring our economic policies into consonance with our technical processes in order that no such treason to human need shall inform our national policy.

We shall give less attention to an artificial fixing of prices and more attention to an authentic freeing of the powers of business, industry, and agriculture to create new wealth from which alone we can provide adequate buying power for consumers and adequate profit for producers.

We shall, in short, lay the foundations for a workable economics of plenty.

We shall deal liberally with our enterprises of scientific research and social education, demanding from their directors in return a conscious consideration of the peculiar problems that give this particular phase of our national evolution both its distinction and its difficulties.

We shall, because we sense the intimate relation between a vital religion and a valid social order, seek to stimulate a religion that lives in the day-to-day affairs of men, and to develop a social order which, by its agreeable impact upon the lives of men, will incline them to believe in a universe instinct with meaning and thereby invest their lives with a sustaining confidence.

We shall make politics the servant instead of the sovereign of our life and enterprise.

We shall attempt, with a statesmanship that goes beyond opportunism and divests itself of chauvinism, realistically to relate economic America to the modern economic world.

These are among the issues with which responsible leadership must deal if the national future is not to be open to the allurements of irresponsible

[246]

leadership which, in reckless willingness to try anything once even if historic experience has repeatedly proved its futility, will promise the moon to the millions in return for a handful of votes.

EPILOGUE

THE DISORDER OF OUR WILL

I HAVE sought to define the major alternatives between which, it seems to me, destiny demands that we choose. In dealing with these alternatives, I have done no more than to state and to emphasize the point of view that, in each instance, seems soundest to me. I have not attempted to buttress my beliefs with a vast array of data. This volume is a tract rather than a treatise, a document of appeal respecting issues that require of the business and political intelligence of the country searching judgment and swift decision.

I have sought to identify the forces of policy and action that are bringing us unavoidably to a turn in the road where we must make a few fundamental decisions if, as I put it at the outset, we are to avoid economic chaos, stabilize and make socially viable our industrial system, and through it all preserve a way of life congenial to the American temperament. I am not at all sure how brilliantly we shall survive this ordeal of choice. Despite the rapidity with which events are educating us, we have still to prove that we are equal to the challenge of these decisions. We are still halting between two opinions. On the basic issues I have discussed, we have yet to give either the Lord or Baal a clear vote.

We have been afflicted, in the secret recesses of our minds, with a paralyzing indecision as we have faced the clashing concepts, contradictory desires, conflicting tendencies, and competing forces that converge in the affairs of our time. We have suffered from that disintegration of will Guglielmo Ferrero so trenchantly diagnosed in his *Words to the Deaf* about a decade ago.

"There have been epochs more uncouth, poorer, and more ignorant than our own," he wrote, "but they knew what they wanted." Their ideas may have been limited, but their wills were sure. "What do we want?" he asked. And then went on to say, "That is the essential question. Every man and every epoch should keep this question constantly before them, just as a lamp is kept burning day and night in dark places."

Ferrero is right. This is the essential question. To know what we want is the beginning of statesmanship. Do we know what we want? Here in the United States? Now? Do we know what we want government to be and do in relation to the whole mechanism and movement of American life and enterprise over which, at its moment of highest potential power, the shadow of a vast futility fell? Do we know what we want from statesmanship? Have we a clear conception of the role of the state in the affairs of the time, or, at the end of a century of science, are we confessing confusion and reverting to rule of thumb in things political? Is our seeming attempt at mastery in reality a disguised drift, with the power of politics increasing as the certainty of statesmanship dwindles? Do we, in short, know what kind of political order we want? Do we know what kind of social order we want? Do we know what kind of economic order we want? Ferrero thinks not.

"On the contrary," he wrote, "our will is in a state of complete confusion. Sometimes it is split in twain, at once desirous of good and evil, or of benefits that are mutually exclusive. Sometimes it cloaks itself in agreeable falsehoods, persuading itself that it desires one thing, while all the time it desires something different or even antithetical. Sometimes it entirely strays away from reason and reality, lured on by a chimerical mirage."

This disorder of the will, Ferrero thinks, is the disease from which our age is dying. Certainly it is a malaise that has relaxed our capacity and dulled our clarity in the field of social decision. We must find medicines that will rid us of this malaise. We cannot make the decisions demanded of us at this juncture in American affairs unless we shake ourselves free from this paralyzing indecision of will.

I should be sorry if this study led anyone to a negative or pessimistic attitude toward the issues of government and enterprise with which it deals. It is important that, in our candid facing of realities, we do not cut the nerve of confident attack. The spirit of confident attack, however, must be deeply rooted in reality. It dies in the thin soil of that insouciant optimism that sometimes seeks to sub-stitute cheer-leading for statesmanship. There is, in fact, always a strain of pessimism in a truly valid and productive optimism. It has faced the worst in order that it may the more intelligently fashion the best. It is this fusion of the two that produces leaderships able to call nations to repentance with-out taking hope from their hearts, to condemn dead policies without deadening the spirit of living enterprise, and to create confidence without cul-tivating illusions.

A while ago I stole away for two weeks to let new sights and new sounds wash out of my mind the tire from long months of routine and responsi-bility. I was but forty-eight hours away from the day's work before the desert reaches of Colorado and New Mexico had administered their anodyne. I began to feel a sense of quiet and perspective I had not known for months. But even the desert talked to me of the affairs with which this study has reckoned.

At first, the desert darkened my mood.

My drawing room, the diner, and the club cars of the train on which I was riding were last words in the sophisticated service of modern and metro-politan America. But the train itself was speeding through long stretches of desolation that gave the lie to the civilization it symbolized. Sterile sand. Scrubby sage brushes. Chalky white patches of alkali dotting the earth. Scrawny horses, their ribs showing, wandering dejectedly, and rubbing their necks against intermittent posts. Slattern cabins, here occupied and there falling into ruin, with no visible contact with civilization. The human scene was no better. Here and there were dull-eyed Mexicans of the peon sort, little knots of workmen, obviously from the ranks of the least skilled, without light in their faces, and Indian remnants of a once regal race. A few days before I had been chatting with representative leaders in business, industry, and finance in a great city. A few days earlier I had been at the center of a great university with its scholarship, its culture, and its eager aliveness to the issues of the time. And yet, the desert reminded me, the wisest man I knew in this great university and the most far-sighted economic statesman I knew in this great city had but one vote, as had each of the occupants of these desolate desert cabins. Had democracy any magic that could scramble the votes of all these in a hat and bring wisdom out? As this question scurried across my mind, the desert darkened my outlook.

A moment later the desert lifted my spirit and brightened my outlook.

For miles the bleak countryside had been brown and baked. Green was a color it had not known. Suddenly the train surged into a run of miles in which dwarf cedars defied the desert with their green. Life lifted its head above death in these cedars. They were dwarfed but defiant. They would not be denied their right to be green. They shook their fists in the face of sand and sun. They would grow and they would be green. They dared drought to down them. They shouted the indestructibility of the will to live, to be, to grow, to bring life out of death, to bring beauty out of barrenness.

This indestructible will to live and to master the stubborn factors of environment, so vividly symbolized by these desert cedars, is resident in the American genius. In this will we shall face the future with courage and bring to the decisions demanded of us a resolute realism of policy.

INDEX